D0345982

WA T

Decide to Win

**This book is to be returned on or before
the last date stamped below.**

FEB 97	3 0 SEP 1997	4 DEC 199
	1 0 MAR 1998	
3. MAY	OT 31 MAR	0 6 APR 200
	12 May ET	2 7 APR 200
MAY		2 9 NOV 2003
	20. JUN	-7 JAN 2004
28. MAY		2 5 MAY
1 1 JUN 1997	1 1 JUL 1998	0 AUG 2004
26. JUN	2 JUL 1998	1 9 JAN 2005
02 AUG		9 FEB 2005
12. SEP		

SUTTON LEISURE SERVICES

WALLINGTON L
Shotfield, Walli
SM6 0HY
0181-770-49

29 MAR 2003   RENEWALS   Please quote:
date of return, your tick
computer label number

0 4 JUN 2005

1 0 SEP 2005

2 2 FEB 2006

2 4 MAY 2006

- 9 NOV 2007

- 9 NOV 2007

17 DEC   DX

Decide to Win

A Total Approach to Winning in
Sport & Life

David Swindley and Rex Johnson

WARD LOCK

SUTTON LEISURE
LIBRARIES
01798693⸝
JAN 1997

A WARD LOCK BOOK

First published in the UK 1996
by Ward Lock

Wellington House 125 Strand LONDON WC2R 0BB

A Cassell Imprint

Copyright © David Swindley and Rex Johnson 1996

All rights reserved. No part of this publication may be reproduced in any
material form (including photocopying or storing it in any medium by
electronic means and whether or not transiently or incidentally to some
other use of this publication) without the written permission of the
copyright owner, except in accordance with the provisions of the Copyright,
Designs and Patents Act 1988 or under the terms of a licence issued
by the Copyright Licensing Agency, 90 Tottenham Court Road,
London W1P 9HE. Applications for the copyright owner's written
permission to reproduce any part of this publication should be
addressed to the publisher.

Distributed in the United States
by Sterling Publishing Co., Inc.
387 Park Avenue South, New York, NY 10016-8810

Distributed in Australia
by Capricorn Link (Australia) Pty Ltd
2/13 Carrington Road, Castle Hill NSW 2154

A British Library Cataloguing in Publication Data block for this book
may be obtained from the British Library

ISBN 0 7063 7533 5

Typeset by Keystroke, Jacaranda Lodge, Wolverhampton
Printed and bound in Great Britain by
Hartnolls Limited, Bodmin, Cornwall

Contents

Acknowledgements

We would like to express our gratitude to Colleen Johnson for editing our draft text, Brian Swindley for innumerable helpful comments and suggestions, and Pam Hanley for her invaluable support and encouragement.

Foreword

The inspiration for writing this book came to us several summers ago. The soccer World Cup was taking place in the USA without British national teams, who had failed to qualify. The England cricket team was being subjected to yet another humiliation against the Australians. British tennis players were suffering their annual early exit from the Wimbledon tennis championships.

We wondered why we Brits could no longer take victory for granted against the smaller nations that were once regarded as second division material. If Norway and the Republic of Ireland can qualify for the soccer World Cup, why not us? If Sweden and the Czech Republic can produce such fine tennis players, why can't we? What did the small, impoverished former Republic of East Germany, which dominated world athletics for so long, do that we couldn't? New Zealand and South Africa have such fearsome rugby players, where are ours? Why has there not been a British Wimbledon men's finalist, yet alone champion, since World War II? Why have we only had one World Champion in 20 years in Formula One motor racing, a sport once dominated by British drivers? Do we really have to rely on the less physical pastimes such as snooker and darts to bolster our national pride?

We pondered on what it takes to be a winner in sport. We reflected on our own experiences in sport and personal development and as motivational consultants, psychotherapists and health practitioners. Our professional activities bring us into contact with people with a wide range of interests, all looking for improvement in some aspect of their lives, many searching for excellence in their chosen fields. Among these are many sportsmen and women. Between us we have worked with more than 20,000 people over nearly a quarter of a century.

We studied the training methods used around the world, including the USA, former Soviet Union, Western Europe, South Africa and Australia. We came to a firm conclusion: physical training, nutrition, technique and talent are all important, but most winning takes place in the mind. Take two teams or individuals with similar physical attributes, and the one with the most

7

positive attitude and emotions will win. So we investigated further. Are these characteristics that people are born with, or can they be developed? If so, how?

We discovered thick volumes on sports psychology tucked away in university libraries, of interest to academics but too expensive and too technical for most people to understand. In contrast, we found slim booklets of the *Play Better Golf/Tennis* variety that covered the basic skills but omitted the most important ones – the mental and emotional. We looked for books that explained the principles in simple terms. We spoke to physical education teachers and sports coaches, all of whom confirmed our suspicions: no such books existed. The material was simply not available in a form that was easily accessible to the average sports enthusiast.

But now it is. Read this book and apply what you learn and you will find a significant improvement in your performance taking place almost immediately. Whether your ambitions are to win your club trophy, represent your region, become world champion, or simply to take part and get more enjoyment from your sport, you will find *Decide to Win* invaluable. And because the qualities needed to win at sport are the same as those required to be successful in any area of your life, you will find it helps you to achieve all the health, happiness and success you desire.

David Swindley and Rex Johnson
Bournemouth, UK

Be a Sport and Come Alive!

*Some people think sport is a matter of life and death. I
don't like that attitude. I can assure them it is much more
important than that.*

With apologies to Bill Shankly, Liverpool football manager

Long ago, two tribes were about to go to war over a piece of land when the
first chief had an idea. Instead of fighting, they would have an archery contest.
The winners would claim the land and nobody would get hurt. This way, this
squabble was settled and, what's more, the chiefs became firm friends and the
tribes never went to war again.

This legend illustrates how sport has always played an important part in
people's lives. The Ancient Greeks understood this. The Romans, too, loved
their sport; the exciting (and gruesome) spectacle of gladiators pitting their
skills against each other thrilled onlookers all over the Roman Empire. In the
Middle Ages, jousting and archery contests were the main attractions at
the annual pageants that took place. Then the Victorians invented the rules
for games such as rugby, cricket and soccer, games which are still popular
today. In the USA, baseball, basketball and American football command
enormous followings. The Australians and New Zealanders are sports mad.
Everywhere, people run, swim and jump in competition with each other.

What's more, national pride is closely tied to a nation's sporting prowess.
People feel good when their country's heroes are doing well and they invent
all sorts of excuses when they're not. We British have heard most of them. The
weather's too unpredictable; the Government doesn't put in enough money;
our administrators are too old-fashioned or bureaucratic; we can't afford the
most up-to-date facilities; we don't pay our top athletes enough; we don't
abuse drugs as much as some other countries; nor do we 'brainwash' our most
promising youngsters and deprive them of a 'normal' childhood.

The excuses go on and on. Are they valid? Perhaps some of them are. Are
the grapes sour? Who knows, we've never tasted them. But we'd like to
suggest something so important that even money and the weather pale into
insignificance by comparison: pride and passion, the competitive spirit, a
sense of achievement, team spirit. In short, our attitude to winning and losing.

If you give up without ever having won, you are where you
were at the beginning – a loser.

M. Scott Peck, author

It is said that we British are much too easily satisfied with a good perform-ance, happy to come second as long as we feel we've done our best in the circumstances. We resent a winner and admire a gallant loser. We love to destroy our heroes once they become 'too' successful. Why? Is there really any sense to this attitude?

The truth is, most of us, even we Brits, love to compete. We all like to win, especially the young. Think about it for a moment. If you want to persuade a 5-year-old to do something, what do you do? You say 'I bet you can't do that' or 'I'll race you'. You make it a challenge and off they go. Sometimes, you let them win because you know it's so important to them.

So here's the big question. How do we manage to convert tenacious young competitors into a nation of losers? What happens between the ages of 5 and 18 years that saps healthy girls and boys of their will to improve, compete and win? Perhaps we should take a look at what happens in our schools. Do they still take competitive sport seriously in the face of ever-increasing academic and vocational demands? Surely schools want to encourage every child to develop their abilities to the full?

Not always. In the UK, we've seen enormous changes in educational philosophies in the last 30 years and priorities are constantly changing. Here's one example. In the mid 1980s, some London schools decided to emphasize participation and fun in their sports lessons. One went as far as changing the rules to make sure nobody lost. In cricket, for example, each 'batsperson' received exactly the same number of balls, regardless of how many times he/she was out. The philosophy was simple enough: all children were to be treated equally, there must be no such thing as winning and losing, and nobody must be made to feel like a failure.

Now, was that school doing those children any favours? What lesson were they supposed to learn? That the world is fair? That everyone always gets a sporting chance in life, irrespective of their abilities or the effort they put in? That nobody ever achieves any more than anyone else? Are these propositions true? Of course not!

Life *is* competitive and young people who learn to compete at games are better equipped for the rough and tumble. This doesn't mean to say that it should or shouldn't be this way, only that it is. If you run your life accord-ing to 'shoulds' and 'shouldn'ts', you're setting yourself up for constant disappointment. If you can cope with losing as well as winning, and pick yourself up and start all over again, you've learned a very important lesson: we can all make the most of our talents, whatever they may be. Success is there for *all* of us, provided that we are willing to apply ourselves.

> *Losing is not always a bad thing, as it means someone else has won. And I think, invariably, learning to accept defeat helps you to be a better person.*
>
> Alan Murphy, PE teacher

Fortunately, that London school's approach was not widely copied. Most good teachers (and parents) understand the value of competition in sport. They know it develops self-esteem, encourages self-discipline and creates confidence. They realize that it has spin-offs into other areas, such as academic studies and the world of work. They believe in winning but also understand losing. And they also believe in participation, encouraging the winners to help the others and the others to keep trying and do their best. None of this, though, prevents sports teachers (and headteachers!) gaining immense satisfaction from seeing teams they have coached drubbing the opposition.

Of course, every boy and girl should be encouraged to take part. If you want to see a wonderful example of young people participating for the sake of sheer enjoyment, pay a visit to our home town, Bournemouth, any Saturday morning from September to May. Go and see Littledown Juniors, the 'biggest football club in the country' in action. It is a truly heartwarming sight to see a dozen matches taking place on adjacent pitches, the youngsters giving it their all while parents cheer them on from the touchline. Founded by a soccer-crazy cleric, the Revd David Wiseman, it has 1,200 members, aged from 6 to 14 years old, boys and girls, divided into 120 teams. There are 11 leagues and two cup competitions within the club; nevertheless the object is not primarily to win but to do your best and have fun.

The club philosophy was once summed up by Revd Wiseman in a newsletter. 'Over the years,' he wrote, 'I have become tired of the "win at all costs" type of player.' He went on to quote Linford Christie, who said, 'As far as I'm concerned, the man who said "it's not the winning that matters but the taking part" was a loser.' 'WRONG, MR CHRISTIE,' wrote Revd Wiseman. 'All our children are achievers because they take part, and the result of the game doesn't matter.'

We are great fans of Littledown Juniors, not least because our sons, Danny, Darren and Joe, are enthusiastic members. We certainly like to see young people encouraged to take part in sport and, these days, there is no excuse for any child wanting to duck out. In recent years, the range of sports offered in UK schools has been broadened considerably so that everyone can choose an activity to their liking. In our local secondary schools, for example, students can play traditional games, such as football, rugby, netball and hockey, and also take up newer options, such as windsurfing, orienteering and cyclo-cross. There is something for everybody, whatever their interests.

But there is a problem with this approach. What should we do for the child who wants to excel, whose ambitions extend beyond a jog around a tame cross-country course once a week? Shouldn't children who have the ability and the desire be given every encouragement to do the very best they can? Shouldn't we make sure the equipment and facilities and coaching they need are provided? Of course. We must support our high achievers in every way we can. But this dictates specialization. It is simply not possible to achieve excellence in a wide range of activities.

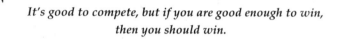

> *It's good to compete, but if you are good enough to win,*
> *then you should win.*
>
> John Isaacs, athletics coach

When we look at the next generation, it seems we have much more to worry about than what they do in sports lessons. What is more alarming is the change in lifestyle among the young. Today's teenagers are the least physically active ever. Research shows that 60 per cent take as little exercise as they can. When the British Heart Foundation studied 11- to 16-year-olds over a 4-day period, they found that an astonishing 78 per cent of youngsters did not experience a single 20-minute period of exercise equal to a brisk walking pace during the 4 days. Today's schoolchildren would obviously rather receive a computer game in their Christmas stocking than a tennis racket or a pair of running shoes.

What a pity! They're missing out on activities which could enrich every area of their lives, both now and in the future. Success on the sports field builds self-belief, a much-needed quality and the foundation stone of achievement. When mind and body are fully integrated, anything is possible.

Tennis coach David Emery once said: 'Anyone can do anything given the right motivation. Too many people think talent alone makes a champion. You also have to have drive.' And here lies the secret of success in any field – motivation, enthusiasm, attitude. In short, mental toughness.

Twenty years ago, professional sport was beginning to witness a new development, one that was treated with scepticism and even derision by many sports enthusiasts. In tennis, it was the young Martina Navratilova who first brought it to people's attention. Her rivals spotted a psychologist travelling with her, along with her coach, a nutritionist and the rest of her entourage. At first they laughed but, when she began winning everything in sight, they sat up and took notice. They knew, of course, that the difference between top players and the rest was confidence, concentration and the ability to handle pressure. In other words, it was mental and emotional, and who could help them in this area? Who other than psychologists?

Today, sports psychologists are widely consulted in many countries. In the USA, Australia and Eastern Europe they have a prominent role to play in any training programme. When the Berlin Wall was breached, it was found that the training techniques used by the East German athletes were classified as top secret. They included a system of mental training that featured deep relaxation, gentle Baroque music and mental rehearsal originally developed by a Bulgarian psychiatrist, Dr Georgi Lozanov. His contribution goes a long way towards explaining the sporting success enjoyed by the Soviet bloc in recent decades.

Nowadays, mental toughness training has come of age and its influence has spread well beyond Soviet athletes and American tennis stars. For example, members of the England Ladies' cricket team, which won the World Cup in 1993, consulted a university sports psychologist during their preparations. Although sceptical at first (indeed, some initially thought it a complete waste of time), they grew to appreciate the benefits. Their opponents in the final, Australia, certainly noticed the improvement and were anxious to discover what had made such a difference to the English players.

The advantages that the Australians were so keen to acquire can now be yours. Why spend years learning by trial and error when you can tap into existing knowledge? Why rely solely on your experience as you strive to improve when you can profit from the practical wisdom shared by those who have already been there and done it? Obviously the gap between victory and defeat in the highest echelons of sport is extremely narrow – an extra 1 or 2 per cent can make the difference between appearing in an Olympic Final and winning a medal – but a 20 or 30 per cent improvement is available to you, right now. The principles and practices in this book apply to you no less than world champions.

Sports psychology is largely common sense but not yet common practice. Average sports enthusiasts are still largely unaware of what it can do for them, but this is changing. You can start today. Remember, the farmer who forgets to sow the seed, or can't be bothered, will have no crop when harvest time comes. Follow the example of the successful farmers. Start sowing now and look forward to a bumper harvest – your performances improving steadily as your confidence grows and your results getting better and better.

Sport is truly a microcosm of life. Like life, it is there to be enjoyed and the qualities you need to be successful are largely the same. Build those qualities into yourself, with our help, and reap the rewards. You can decide to win at sport and the game of life. It's entirely up to you.

In life there are many opportunities, and too many people who never see them. Then there are the winners. They see the opportunities, they go looking for them, and that's what you're facing now. Go and take the opportunity, it's there for you.

Graham Taylor, former England soccer manager

Anatomy of a Winner

*Sports do not build character
– they reveal it.*

Heywood Broun

Cyclist Greg Lemond's victory in the 1989 Tour de France was one of the most remarkable ever. Two years earlier, he had suffered a freak hunting accident which left him lying in a field, riddled with lead shotgun pellets, gasping for breath and wondering if he would ever see his family again. As if this wasn't bad enough, 4 months after the accident his appendix was removed. A year later he underwent surgery on his leg, which forced him to miss the 1988 Tour de France. Meanwhile, his team managers lost faith in him and terminated his contract. Then he was found to be suffering from anaemia. He wondered if his days as a top-flight cyclist were over.

But Lemond was not a quitter. Even in the depths of despair he carried on training. Since the leading teams were no longer interested, he signed for a less prestigious outfit. He gradually began to feel stronger. By the time the 1989 Tour came round, he believed he had a realistic chance of finishing in the top 20. He felt invigorated by the supercharged atmosphere of the event, got off to a good start and finished fourth in the opening stage. By the end of the fifth day, he was in the lead but he lost ground to his great rival, Laurie Fignon, in the gruelling mountain stages and, on the eve of the final stage, was in second place, 50 seconds behind. This was a huge margin, more than anyone had ever made up before. No one, including the over-confident Fignon, gave him a chance, especially since his body was still peppered with lead pellets. No one, that is, except Lemond himself. In a breathtaking race, which culminated in a high-speed dash through the streets of Paris, he covered the final stage flat out to take the title for the second time, an incredible 58 seconds faster than Fignon.

The moral of this story is crystal clear. With effort, determination and persistence, anything is possible. Yes, anything. Here's another example.

A young boy in the poorest district of San Francisco had an ambition to become a great American footballer, just like his hero, Cleveland's Jim Brown. One day, when Cleveland were in town to play the San Francisco 49-ers, the boy bumped into Jim Brown in a café. 'Mr Brown,' he said excitedly, 'I'm your biggest fan. I know every record you've ever set, every touchdown you've ever scored. And one day, I'm going to break every one of your records.'

Brown smiled. Who knows what he was thinking as he looked at the boy, crippled with rickets, his legs bowed, walking with a limp. But he responded encouragingly. 'That's great, kid. What's your name?'

'Orenthal James Simpson,' the boy replied. 'My friends call me O. J.'

Against all the odds, O. J. Simpson did go on to break every one of Jim Brown's records. It seems incredible that such a boy could go on to become an all-time great in a game as rough and demanding as American football but he wasn't the only disadvantaged youngster to make the grade in professional sport. In some ways children from deprived backgrounds have an advantage. Sport can offer a way out of poverty for dedicated youngsters the world over, so underprivileged children have a huge incentive. Pelé and Eusebio, two of the greatest footballers ever, were so poor they had to perfect their skills using any suitable discarded object they could find. Geoff Boycott, who scored over 48,000 runs in 20 years as one of the world's top cricketers, learned to bat in a muddy alley using a rubbish bin as a wicket. Even in those days the other boys couldn't get him out; they would give up and go home.

The truth is, the qualities you need to be a winner have little to do with origin, money or privilege. Whatever your background, if you develop the right qualities you can make it. What are these qualities? Why don't you take a few moments to think about them and list them on a piece of paper. Then compare your list with ours.

Winning qualities

Desire

Desire is the stuff of champions. It is wanting to win so badly that you'd do anything (legal, that is) to achieve your goal. Without desire, there's no incentive to put in all the hard work that is necessary. With desire, you can overcome all obstacles.

Angela Mullinger is a woman in her late 30s who runs for our local athletic club. She desperately wanted to compete in the 10th World Veterans' Athletics Championships in Japan in October 1993 but did not have the money she needed for the air fare and accommodation. Her employers contributed £450 but that was £2,000 short of the total. What made it harder to bear was that one of her team mates had found a sponsor willing to cover the whole cost.

What did Angela do? Was she tempted to follow the old adage, 'If at first you don't succeed, give up?' Not a bit of it; her desire was too strong. She talked her bank manager into lending her the money and, to her delight, won two gold medals and a silver.

Desire is the foundation stone of success. If you feel you can't muster enough of it at the moment, don't worry. We've plenty of suggestions for intensifying your desire in the following chapters.

Enthusiasm and passion

When we watch two equally talented and dedicated competitors, which one do we usually support? Usually the one with the most enthusiasm, the most passion. Passion is one half of the equation that produces unstoppable motivation. Passion and purpose, together, *are* motivation.

In Chapter 3, you will find out how to turn your desire into concrete goals and a comprehensive training plan. However, there's no point in doing any of this unless you are enthusiastic because otherwise it will become a hard slog. If the enthusiasm isn't there, you may as well admit to yourself that you'd be better off devoting your time to something else.

Determination and persistence

If you want to see determination in action, watch a top sprinter like Linford Christie. When he is preparing to race, his face epitomizes the power of determination and concentration. He focusses on the winning tape, imagining he's already there even before the starting pistol is fired. He is also a model of persistence. Christie was beaten 12 out of 13 times by his great rival, Carl Lewis, prior to winning a gold medal at the 1992 Olympic Games. Many commentators thought that, at 33 years old, he'd missed his chance but he simply refused to give up.

Many talented sportsmen and women have given up without ever achieving all they could, which is a pity. There's nothing more pointless than dropping out as you round the final bend; you may never know just how near you were to the winning post. Without determination and persistence, you might win a few minor victories but you certainly won't reach your full potential.

> *Nothing in the world can take the place of persistence.*
> *Talent will not; nothing is more common than*
> *unsuccessful men and women of talent. Genius will not;*
> *unrewarded genius is almost a proverb. Education will not;*
> *the world is full of educated derelicts. Persistence and*
> *determination alone are omnipotent.*

Calvin Coolidge, President of the USA (1872–1933)

Resilience

Many great sports stars have been knocked down so often, it's a miracle some of them ever bounced back. Probably the most incredible comeback of recent time was that of the Austrian tennis player, Thomas Muster, whose nickname in tennis circles is 'The Miracle Man'. In April 1989, Muster, the world-ranking Number Six, was hit by a drunken driver and his left leg was crushed. As he was rushed into hospital, it seemed he would never walk again but, astonishingly, a mere 10 days after final surgery, Muster was back on a tennis court, suspended in a harness and with his left leg in plaster, practising. It was the start of a recovery which would eventually see him reach Number One in the world and continue to be among the world's best tennis players for many years.

Winners follow the old Japanese proverb 'Fall down seven times, stand up eight!' They shrug off the inevitable disappointments and keep their eye firmly on the goal.

The greatest success is not in never falling,
but in rising every time you fall.

Vince Lombardi, American football coach (1913–70)

Concentration

Concentration is the ability to focus your attention on the task in hand and without it you're not going to get very far. How can you possibly win if your mind is wandering? Big matches have been won and lost solely because someone was able to keep his or her concentration better than the other. A boxer who can't concentrate will be knocked out. A racing driver will crash. A goalkeeper will find himself continually picking the ball out of the net. An ice skater will fall. Need we say more?

All the advantages of thorough preparation will be lost if you're unable to be totally, 100 per cent 'there' in mind and body, concentrating fully on what you're doing.

Confidence

It's hard to think of a single champion who lacks confidence – not necessarily the loud and brash variety but the quiet assurance that you can and will win. Confidence isn't something you are born with. When you are born you neither have confidence nor lack confidence: you either learn to behave confidently or you don't.

If you feel lacking in confidence, you should realize that you can decide to build it into yourself, provided that you're willing to put in a little effort, using the techniques you'll read about in later chapters. You'll feel better about yourself in all areas of your life as your self-esteem rises.

> *An Olympic swimmer has to get up on the block and make probably one of the most sublimely arrogant state-ments:*
> *'I am the best in the world' – and believe it one hundred and ten percent.*
>
> Duncan Goodhew, Olympic breast-stroke gold medallist

Positive attitude

What exactly do we mean by *positive attitude*? We would sum it up in three short phrases: positive desire, self-belief and positive expectancy. These three, backed up with self-discipline, pave the way to positive results.

Positive people always focus on the good in any situation, are optimistic yet realistic and refuse to allow discouragement to creep in, whatever the situation. For example, the racing driver Nigel Mansell has all these qualities and more. As a young man, nobody else believed he could make it but his resolve stayed firm. For 12 years he suffered serious injury, financial hardship and appalling luck. On many occasions he raced wearing a surgical contraption to hold his neck in place, relying on painkillers to subdue the agony. His car kept breaking down, even when he appeared to have victory sewn up. Critics and fans alike derided him. They said he was too cocky, made too many mistakes and was full of excuses, but this only made him more determined. He always believed that he could win the championship if he could find the right car, and this proved to be the case.

Another example of an unshakeable positive attitude is a local athlete we much admire, Chris Brogan. He can often be seen training along the sea-front in Bournemouth and he competes annually in the London Marathon, clocking times as low as 2 hours 40 minutes. His fitness is such that his pulse reading, at rest, is only 45 beats per minute.

Yet Chris is confined to a wheelchair after a tragic abseiling accident. He recalls the moment when it dawned on him that he would never be able to walk again. 'Damn, I don't want to sit on my backside for the rest of my life,' he said to himself. 'I've got to do something about it.' Chris and thousands of other disabled athletes show what can be done and provide an object lesson to us all.

Courage

Have you ever marvelled at the sheer nerve of ski jumpers, hurtling down those huge ramps at speeds of up to 145 kilometres (90 miles) an hour, then hovering for what seems like an eternity before landing smoothly and gliding gracefully to a halt? In ski jumping, all the skill in the world cannot compensate for a lack of daring and, in many other sports too, physical courage is an absolute necessity. In boxing, there has recently been a spate of worrying injuries and, in motor sport, many have died pursuing their world championship dreams. You need guts in ball games such as cricket and rugby. Can you imagine being tackled by an All Black prop forward, or facing up to a West Indian fast bowler? The very thought of it turns most people's knees to jelly. And how about figure skating? It takes courage to spin round on the ice at lightning speed, knowing that one bad landing could rupture your ankle ligaments or shatter a knee joint in an instant.

It also takes courage to excel at games such as darts, snooker and chess, but this is courage of a different kind – *mental* courage, which is the willingness to put yourself on the line. Take snooker, hardly a game requiring physical courage. Players often face situations where potting a ball could win the match but missing would hand the frame to their opponent. Remember the famous final between Steve Davis and Dennis Taylor in 1985 where the world championship rested on the final black?

Courage is not an absence of fear but going ahead anyway in spite of it. The main fear which holds most people back is the fear of failure. You must never be afraid to fail because, if you play it safe, you will never improve and failure can teach you valuable lessons. Do you think Ian Botham would have taken as many wickets as he did by concentrating on economy, or scored as many runs by resorting to defence? Of course not! He was willing to risk being caught on the boundary or hit for six, knowing that the ultimate rewards would be worth it. Sport, and life, can be compared to fruit picking. If you want the best, you must be prepared to go out on a limb sometimes, because that is where you'll find the most fruit.

Patience and dedication

Rome wasn't built in a day and neither are champions. They have to work hard to build the winning qualities into themselves and it doesn't happen overnight. They suffer setbacks and experience false starts but treat them as stepping stones to success.

Your long-term aspirations demand patience. So does your performance on match day. Great champions, such as Chris Evert and Björn Borg, were known for it; so were Geoff Boycott and Steve Davis. Patiently grinding down an opponent can be much more successful than going all out in the early stages and running out of steam. Once the opponent gets frustrated and discouraged you can pounce with a killer blow; remember Ali versus Foreman in the World Heavyweight contest in 1974?

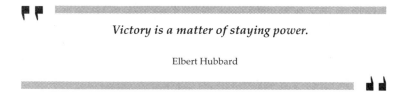

Victory is a matter of staying power.

Elbert Hubbard

A sense of fun

Wouldn't life be dull if we didn't enjoy what we were doing? Laughter and a sense of fun adds to our happiness and increases our sense of well-being. It contributes to physical health, increases injury recovery rates and inspires the people around us. Legend has it that Matt Busby, the manager of the great Manchester United football teams of the 1940s, 1950s and 1960s, would send his teams out on to the field with the words, 'Go out and enjoy yourselves'. It must have worked. His teams won, among other things, five league championships, two FA Cups and a European Cup!

We hope you've thought about the qualities *you* need to be a winner as you've read this chapter. The next step is to decide to build them into yourself. You'll have to work at it, of course, with a positive attitude, but it will be worth it. There is invariably a price to be paid for any success. But as John F. Kennedy once remarked, the price of action is always far less than the cost of 'comfortable inaction'.

Goals – the Secret of Motivation

Whatever your mind can conceive and believe,
you can achieve.

Dynamic Living Principle No. 5

What is it that separates outstanding champions from the rest? What magic quality do they have that makes them stand out? Talent? Certainly, although the sports history books are littered with talented individuals who never became great champions (Ilie Nastase, Jimmy White and Rodney Marsh to name but three). Strength? Perhaps, depending on the sport, but many times the smaller person has triumphed over a larger, stronger opponent – remember how Muhammad Ali first won the World Heavyweight Boxing title against the brutish man-mountain, Sonny Liston. Luck? Definitely not. As Gary Player, the great South African golfer once pointed out, the harder he practised, the luckier he got.

No, what distinguishes the greats from the also-rans is their burning desire – desire which impels them to train, dedicate themselves, practise, compete . . . and win.

Ask yourself: 'If I were guaranteed the highest honour in my sport – a gold medal, the world championship, to be part of a world-cup winning side or whatever – in exchange for so many hours hard work every day, how many hours would I train?

The answer reveals how serious you are about your sport. If it is 5, 6 hours or more, you're in earnest. All the top stars had to put in this amount of time to get to the top – and they didn't slack off once they'd got there. The rest of us probably can't spare this amount of time but, whatever your horizons, you'll need to put in enough hours. Anything less than 1 hour a day probably won't be enough.

Whether your ambitions lie on the world stage or the local park, the secret of inner-directed motivation is focussed, determined and persistent goal setting. Anyone who begins to set goals, commits themselves to a plan to work towards them and writes them down and continually thinks about them finds their level of performance improving almost immediately. Not having goals is rather like driving a car without holding the steering wheel. The car veers off the road as if it has a mind of its own. Having goals is like keeping your hands firmly on the wheel. *You* are fully in charge of the direction you are taking.

It won't always be easy. When your friends are off to the pub and you know you still haven't finished your training, you will have to hold fast to your resolve. And it's hard to drag yourself out of bed early on a cold, wet, winter's morning to go for a run, swim or take the horses out for a gallop unless you have a long-term goal. How else can you put up with the short-term discomfort other than reminding yourself of the ultimate success you crave?

> Peter Scudamore is the most successful jockey in steeple-chasing history. He has broken more records than any other National Hunt jockey. In 1989, he won 100 races in less than 5 months, knocking 7 weeks off the previous record. Then he set himself a new goal: to ride more winners in a season than any previous jockey. His total for the season, 221, shattered the previous record of 149, set 10 years earlier. His achievement was even more remarkable because knowledgeable punters considered it impossible to reach 200!

Just in case we haven't yet convinced you of the power of setting goals for yourself, we want to give you one more powerful reason. Don't worry if you don't quite grasp it yet; we'll explain it more fully in Chapter 9.

Your mind consists of a conscious and an unconscious part (see page 74). The conscious contains all the thoughts and feelings you are aware of from minute to minute. The unconscious houses all your memories and habits and is the source of a powerful set of programmes and instincts that control and guide you without your even being aware of it.

Just imagine what would happen if you could direct your unconscious mind to help you to improve your performance! Well, you can, in many different ways, and setting goals is one of the most effective. Once you learn to set goals and commit yourself to achieving them, your unconscious mind gets to work to realize them. It makes you more aware of opportunities to achieve them and brings you a host of creative ideas, insights and images, all aimed at fulfilling your purpose.

Successful goal setting

Nothing gives you a greater feeling of control over your life and a warm glow of satisfaction than setting and achieving progressively more challenging goals. Without them you'll drift, like a ship with a broken rudder at the mercy of the tides. Once you've set goals for yourself, you'll be amazed at how much easier it becomes to focus yourself and keep your motivation sky high.

Successful goal setting in ten easy steps

1 Set a goal you intensely desire.

2 Foster the belief that you can achieve it.

3 Write down your goals and list the benefits that will be yours when you achieve them.

4 Take stock of your present situation and your potential and identify the obstacles you will have to overcome.

5 Prioritize and set deadlines.

6 Assess the resources you will need and the essential qualities you must build into yourself.

7 Make a plan.

8 Use creative imagery to see yourself as if your goal is already achieved.

9 Take action.

10 Monitor your progress and change direction if you aren't getting the results you want.

If you follow our approach to setting goals, your drive towards winning will be irresistible. You will programme your unconscious at a very deep level and astonish yourself and your friends with how quickly your performance improves.

1 Set a goal you intensely desire

You cannot score if you don't know where the goal is: without a goal that you can eagerly commit yourself to, you will dissipate your energy like a scattergun, spraying your shots in all directions and getting nowhere.

The first thing you need to understand is the difference between *achievement* goals and *performance* goals. This isn't too difficult – the words speak for themselves. Achievement goals are what you eventually want to accomplish. If you are really ambitious, they could include winning a major championship, earning £X million pounds, beating the world record time, or anything else that fills you with excitement.

For the rest of us, the principles are exactly the same. If you would be happy if you could make the local team, do better in the tennis club championship or represent your local pub at darts, you can still set achievement goals and follow the process through.

Achievement goals can be long or medium term. Of course, you won't rise from a club player to representing your country in a few months but in 5 years – maybe? Surely you could establish yourself as a regular in the first team in 3 to 6 months if you were determined enough.

If you are only a few days off competing for something you have been working towards for several years, your achievement goal is very short term but it is more usual to be concerned with performance goals in the short term. This is because performance goals keep you posted along the way. They help you to monitor your progress towards your long-term achievement goals. They are concerned with how you want to perform week by week, match by match. They must, of course, be set with your achievement goals in mind so that the accomplishment of each one automatically leads to the realization of the other.

Let's take an example. A young tennis player wants to be selected for the first team of her local club. This is her long-term achievement goal. Meanwhile, she will have to improve her strokes, cultivate the right mental attitude, build her physique and learn to manage her energy levels and recovery time. Every match she plays will give her feedback on how well she is performing. She will know how many times she comes to the net, serves a weak second service or hits a winning forehand drive. She will know how well she keeps her concentration. All these are indications of her level of performance week in, week out.

How can you tell an achievement goal from a performance goal? The answer is quite simple. If you're preparing for a major event and your next race is a training run that you want to do in a certain time to find out whether you're on course, it's a performance goal. If it's the big event itself, it's an achievement goal. And neither have to be earth-shattering to be meaningful. For instance, in a competition between a gifted, experienced player and a novice, the weaker player might set a performance goal simply of winning a minimum number of points or improving on his/her personal best.

Now you have set your goals. Thousands of successful competitors have done the same, yet never made the grade. Why not? Usually, it's because they don't believe they can really do it, which is the next step.

2 Foster the belief that you can achieve it

When Muhammad Ali set himself the goal of becoming the World Heavyweight Boxing Champion he believed beyond a shadow of a doubt that he could and would achieve it. Nigel Mansell had to overcome fierce resistance from his family when he set his goal. They thought he was dreaming his life away and should get a proper job but he clung steadfastly to his belief that he would one day become the World Formula One Motor Racing Champion. Like both these men, you, too, need to believe in yourself and your abilities, or you are giving your opponents a huge advantage.

*A man who doubts himself is like a man who enlists in the
ranks of the enemy and bears arms against himself.
He makes his failure certain by being the
first to be convinced of it.*

Alexandre Dumas, French writer (1824–95)

Here are two ways of building the unshakeable conviction that you can achieve your ambitions. The first is to make your goals credible. In the long term you can achieve anything you like, if you truly believe you can and are willing to put in the time and effort required. But you must also be realistic. You are not going to go from clocking a 5-minute mile this year to running it in under 4 minutes next year. Your unconscious mind will not accept your short-term goals if they are too far beyond your current level of achievement. Make them believable. Then they will be easy to hold in your conscious mind, and your unconscious will embrace them and set to work helping you to bring them about.

The solution is to set goals which have about a fifty-fifty chance of success in the short to medium term. Aim to cut your 5-minute mile to 4 minutes 30 seconds next year. If you scored 500 runs last season, aim for 700 now. If your golf handicap is 20, aim for 16. Your goals should be challenging enough to stretch your abilities, never easy but perfectly possible.

The second way you can build your self-belief is to use the Dynamic Living techniques we have developed to feed your unconscious mind with positive input. Affirmations, creative imagery and positive self-talk are all invaluable. You can convince yourself that the pleasure of achieving your goals will far outweigh the expenditure of time and effort and, yes, the physical discomfort involved.

Above all, you must realize that, unless you enjoy it, there is no point in kidding yourself that you want to excel at sport and are willing to pay the price of success. You can only be really good at what you love to do and, unless you find the whole process pleasurable – every part of it, including the hours of practice, the downs as well as the ups – you won't succeed. So ask yourself: 'Is this what I really want?' If the answer is 'yes', you're on your way.

3 Write down your goals and list the benefits that will be yours when you achieve them

You can add power to your goals and imprint them on your mind by writing them out in detail. Do it every day. The simple act of writing them down reminds your unconscious. We advise you to write them out on a little card that fits easily into a pocket or handbag, so that you can carry them around with you. Then, every time you reach for your wallet or purse, you won't be able to avoid seeing them. Repetition is the key to learning.

There is one more thing you can do to add impact to your goals. Think of all the reasons why you want to achieve your goals, compelling reasons that will drive you forward. Make a list of all the benefits that will come your way through achieving them and all the penalties you will pay if you don't. Conduct a one-person mindstorm. How about the sense of pride? What difference will it make in your life to be known as a winner? What will it do for your self-esteem? Your sex appeal? Your bank balance? The more reasons you can write down, the more powerful will be your motivation.

As the weeks go by, you will probably find yourself adding to your list until you have literally dozens of convincing reasons, every one a push or a pull in the right direction.

4 Take stock of your present situation and your potential and identify the obstacles you will have to overcome

If we dropped you somewhere in Australia with a map and compass and told you to make your way to Sydney, what's the first thing you would want to know? You'd want to know precisely where you are. It's exactly the same with goals. It's no use knowing where you want to get to unless you know where you are right now, then you will know how far you have to travel in your journey and in which direction.

Ask yourself: 'How good am I right now? How fast am I? How fast could I be? What are my physical strengths and weaknesses? My positive and negative mental and emotional qualities?' Be realistic. If you weigh 95 kilograms (15 stones) and are over 1.8 metres (6 feet) tall, you are unlikely to ever be a winning jockey or cox. If you are only 1.6 metres (5 feet 2 inches) tall, basketball is unlikely to be the sport for you and your chances of becoming an effective prop forward are slim.

It is useful to analyse your performance over the past few months and see if you can detect any patterns. Compare yourself with your fellow athletes. How about those whom you would most like to emulate. How big is the gap? What do they do particularly well that you will need to improve upon?

Another worthwhile activity at this point is to consider the stumbling blocks you will have to overcome. Without obstacles you are not challenging yourself very much, so you will not improve. You may need to consider how you will find the time, somewhere to train and the right equipment. Also, if you're aiming high, you'll need a good coach.

Keep your goals to yourself. If you think your friends and family would try to deter you, don't tell them. Nothing is as off-putting as negative comments from other people, but remember, sharing your goals can work the opposite way too. If your loved ones can see how important the goals are to you, and you ask for their practical and moral support, you may get it.

Above all, try to be objective and don't fool yourself. Airy-fairy wishes and hopes will do you no good at all. If you delude yourself that you have no weaknesses, you're hardly likely to be able to eliminate them. And if you are too modest about your strengths, how can you use them as a springboard for greater success?

5 Prioritize and set deadlines

If you've followed our suggestions so far, you'll be clear on what you're trying to achieve and the size of the task facing you. You now need to cultivate a sense of urgency, otherwise you'll find it hard to get started, and there's only one way – decide which of your goals are the most important and set deadlines.

The best way is to work backwards from your long-term goal. When do you intend to achieve it? Some goals are more urgent than others; for example, if you want to be a professional footballer you've probably missed the boat already if you're in your late 20s. If you want to represent your country at an Olympic Games you must aim to peak in the right year. But if your aim is to reduce your golf handicap or run half marathons just for fun, you can take things more leisurely.

Next, decide when you will have to achieve your medium-term goals and, finally, think about the short term, which may be the coming season, the next 3 to 6 months, or whatever seems right for you.

Whatever your time frame, remember you can only build into yourself the qualities you need by taking each day one at a time. It is no use thinking about what you'd like to do 2 years from now if you overlook today's practice! It helps if you are clear on exactly what you have to do today when you get up in the morning. Even if your aim is a modest one, you will lose ground to your rivals if you miss so much as a day's training.

6 Assess the resources you will need and the essential qualities you must build into yourself

Winning at anything means building into yourself the qualities and characteristics you need, so consider what those qualities are. Knowledge? Skills? Physical strength, stamina, suppleness? What equipment will you need? Have you enough money to buy it at present? Will you have to take time off work to get the time you need, or travel out of town to find the right facilities? How important is your family's support? This could be crucial if you are devoting many hours to your training during your leisure time.

Naturally, these depend to some extent on the sport. If you aim to be a top golfer, you will have to join a golf club, employ the coaching services of the resident professional and acquire the right equipment. In golf, all this can be very expensive but there are many sports where finance isn't a major problem. For example, some of the great African runners had little more than a pair of shorts, some old trainers and the dusty streets of their native villages with which to perfect their art.

Whatever the resources you need, we suggest you think carefully about them, write them down and move on to the next step.

7 Make a plan

If you fail to plan, you are planning to fail by default. Without a good map setting out your journey, you'll probably get lost; similarly, without a well-thought-out physical and mental training programme, you risk falling by the wayside.

What should be included in your plan? Quite simply, everything you need to think about, acquire and do to realize your goals. Your plan should be as complete as you can make it with the information you currently have available. Detail everything you need to do, prioritized so you know exactly what needs to be done first, second, third, and so on. Then attach your deadlines and you have your training programme.

But beware: no plan should ever be cast in stone. Circumstances are bound to change, so be prepared to be flexible. If, for instance, you suffer an injury, or have overlooked something, it would be ridiculous to carry on regardless – amend the plan. A well-constructed plan will give you the direction you need, but only if it stays relevant. The one thing you should never do, though, is change the plan just because it seems too much like hard work. Never forget, when the going gets tough, the tough get going!

Success is the progressive realisation of a worthy goal.

Earl Nightingale, writer and broadcaster

8 Use creative imagery to see yourself as if your goal is already achieved

This step provides the magic ingredient that will make your progress towards your goals unstoppable. It's quite simple – just focus your mind on what you want. Hold it in your mind as if you've already done it. See yourself holding the cup, hear the crowd cheering and applauding, hear the announcer proclaiming you as the winner. Summon up those pleasurable feelings of pride and achievement. It feels good, doesn't it?

This is creative imagery in action, a very powerful tool for conditioning your unconscious mind and one about which we'll have much more to say in Chapter 12.

9 Take action

Now you know what you want and have worked out a plan to achieve it, you must go ahead and put it into action with persistence and determination. All the hopes and dreams in the world, and all the best-laid plans, will come to nothing unless you carry them out. The best plan in the world won't work if you don't.

10 Monitor your progress and change direction if you aren't getting the results you want

Taking action isn't the end of it. What if your plan turns out to be imperfect? What if the results you hoped for are not materializing? What if you have fallen behind with your training or failed to meet one of your crucial performance goals?

Naturally, if you feel you are going wrong somewhere, analyse the problem, think of alternative ways of going about your task, choose the best and press on with all the determination and self-discipline you can muster. Winners continually bounce back and keep going, knowing that victory is inevitable if they do.

You've got to have a dream if you're ever going to have a dream come true, and sensible and practical goal setting is the path to fulfilling your sporting dreams. Success is really very easy. All you have to do is decide what you want to accomplish, determine the effort you're willing to put in and resolve to apply yourself. Put in a nutshell like this, it is really very straightforward. Now you're in on the secret, go for it!

Getting Down to Basics

You can have whatever you want in life providing you are
willing to invest the necessary time, energy and effort.

Dynamic Living Principle No. 7

When Bobby Moore was a teenager, his friends would have laughed if anyone had suggested that he would one day lead a team to victory in a World Cup final. They wouldn't even have believed that he could make a professional footballer. Nobody thought 'Tubby' Moore had what it takes – except for one person. He encouraged him to slim down, then build up his physique. He made him practise, hour after hour, kicking, trapping, passing the ball, heading – all the basic skills. He inspired him to study the game until he was a master tactician, so he knew instinctively where to position himself when the opposing team was on the attack. Under this person's guidance, the young Moore learned leadership skills, composure and self-discipline.

Have you guessed the identity of the coach who endowed the future England Captain with all these essential traits? It was Bobby Moore himself. He succeeded solely because he knew what he had to do and then kept going until he'd mastered it.

You'll always find that people who succeed at any activity have done the groundwork. It's undoubtedly the key to success in sport at any level. Rex was well aware of this when he was learning karate. He spent the first 6 weeks learning nothing other than how to fall. In Japan, the home of martial arts, students spend several months simply learning how to make a fist and up to a year mastering the basic punch. Until they are adept at the fundamentals, they are not allowed to go on to more advanced skills.

Ask any professional. Top golfers appreciate the importance of gripping the club correctly. Rugby players spend hours practising handling the ball. Swimmers learn to breathe correctly. Cricketers work on the forward defensive stroke until it is second nature. Can you name a single sport where you can succeed without being thoroughly proficient in the basic techniques? You can't. There isn't one.

Take, for example, the World Snooker Champion, Stephen Hendry. From a very early age, he had a burning ambition to become the world Number One.

He dreamed about it and imagined himself holding the trophy. He practised for 6 hours a day. He went on to become the youngest world champion ever and has since won the title on three further occasions, once while playing with a broken arm. His earnings have topped £3 million but, to Hendry, the money is just a bonus; being the champion and earning his living doing what he enjoys are far more important to him. Do you think he still practises for 6 hours a day, now that he is right at the top of his profession? Of course he does – because he wants to stay there!

Practise yourself, for heaven's sake, in little things;
and thence proceed to greater.

Epictetus, Stoic philosopher and moralist

Sports stars make it look so effortless that you could be forgiven for thinking it's easy; that it's possible to get by on talent, natural ability and flair alone. How misleading; nothing could be further from the truth. Bobby Moore used to make the game look easy but only because he'd spent the time perfecting his skills. Stephen Hendry makes potting a snooker ball look simple but only because he's practised every day for years. Muhammad Ali wouldn't have 'moved like a butterfly, stung like a bee' without dedicating himself to his art throughout his teenage years.

Perhaps you're thinking that what these great sporting heroes have achieved is not really relevant to you. Wrong again. Even if the height of your ambition is to swim for your club in the next local gala, dedication and practice are the keys to improvement. Who do you think will be the best club golfer: one who practises every week or another who only plays once a month? Which runner is more likely to complete the half marathon: one who runs 6 or 7 miles (about 10 kilometres) every day or another who starts training 6 weeks before the event and runs only occasionally when he feels like it?

The key to learning anything is relentless repetition, which results in the creation of brand-new habit patterns in the unconscious. How did you learn to ride a bicycle? There's only one way – doing it over and over again until you've mastered it. But it's no use practising the wrong thing or doing it the wrong way or you may become very proficient at a skill which is relatively unimportant or ignore skills which are vital. If you practise incorrectly you'll simply become very good at doing it wrong. You must find out what you need to be able to do well and practise doing it correctly.

There's a well-known saying that 'Practice makes perfect'. It's a myth.

If you practise making a shot the wrong way, you'll get very good at doing it badly. You won't even have to think about it; doing it the wrong way will be perfectly natural to you. Practice by itself doesn't make perfect. *Practice makes permanent.* And practising perfectly produces permanent perfection!

So where does this leave talent? What is the role of flair and natural ability? There are some sports where it can give you an enormous advantage, such as sprinting. Scientists believe that successful sprinters' muscles are 70 per cent fast-twitch fibre, compared with 50 per cent for the rest of us, and that innate characteristics of their nervous systems enable them to explode out of the starting blocks. If you're born with physical advantages such as these, you're lucky. But even if you're not, you can still improve. Innate ability can always be improved upon; it's a question of how much you want to develop it. Everyone can strive to realize their own, unique potential.

With average talent, you can still become a very good club player – if you have the desire. A person loaded with natural ability can make it right to the very top if they're prepared to work at it. Frank Bruno reached the very top of his profession and became the World Heavyweight Boxing Champion through sheer guts and effort and strength. With the same dedication, Mike Tyson, with all his natural ability, could have been world champion for many years but he became over-confident and allowed his resolve to slip. As this book goes to press, he has recently regained the World Heavyweight Championship from Bruno. If he can maintain the right attitude, there are no limits to what he may achieve.

Talent can often be beaten by tenacity of purpose. When Wimbledon beat the multi-million-pound Liverpool side in the 1988 FA Cup final, it was a triumph for commitment over class and style. Such commitment will always out-do talent alone. We've known relatively ungifted people learn to serve well at tennis, bat and bowl in cricket and execute a creditable tumble turn in swimming through sheer willpower and self-belief. They'll never win the US Open, the Ashes or the Olympics because they didn't set their sights that high, but they will enjoy many hours of pleasure, knowing that they'll give a good account of themselves.

How do we know? Well, we've done it ourselves. When Rex was in his teens and 20s, he played for a local football team. Although, by his own admission, other players had more skill, Rex was the most tenacious member of the team. 'Lofty' Johnson always gave 110 per cent. Later, he took up running. Well into his 40s, and in spite of a visual disability, he completed an 88-kilometre (55-mile) super-marathon. He'll tell you that he had no special talent, just determination, perseverance and enthusiasm.

David hadn't given running a second thought until he saw the London Marathon on television one year. He was so impressed by an elderly woman who finished the course that he bought some running shoes the very next day and, before long, was covering 8 kilometres, 11 kilometres, then 16 kilometres (5, 7 then 10 miles). He bought a book by Bruce Tulloh, the former Olympic long-distance runner, and followed his training plan. Wherever he was, he never missed his daily run and he entered fun runs and half marathons, just for the enjoyment. If he can do it, so can you!

Modelling

Many of our great sporting heroes and heroines learned their trade by trial and error, and yet more error, until they perfected their art, a process that can take many years. If you're smart, you can save yourself a great deal of time and become just as expert by using an approach called *modelling*. Modelling is simply finding out how somebody does something, then adopting their approach. What do winners do that is different from people who are less successful? What is the difference that makes the difference?

To model successfully, you need to do more than just watch and imitate winners. You must get under their skin; see, hear and feel as they do; and adopt their attitudes until you make them your own. What do they pay attention to during their performance? What words and expressions do they use when they talk about their sport? Sports psychologists have concentrated much of their effort on studying top players, identifying their special skills, beliefs and thoughts and then teaching them to promising youngsters. In this way, they can bring them up to international standard much more quickly.

The secret is to find someone who you really admire, then read about them, watch them in as many films and videos as you can, listen to them being interviewed and observe them very carefully. Think about this: if you had to stand in for them for 24 hours, what would you have to do and think to behave like them? How would you go about creating their model of the world in your mind?

If you are fortunate enough to be able to meet them, ask them directly: 'What do you think about when you are about to serve?' 'Why do you stand as you do when about to tee off?' 'When a fast bowler is running in, what's on your mind?' 'Why do you adjust the position of the ball like you do when you're about to take a goal kick?'

Once you've become a good player, you can even model yourself. Cast your mind back to a time when you were really pleased with your performance. How did you feel? What were you saying to yourself? What beliefs about yourself were you holding that particular day? The exciting thing is that you can achieve exactly the same results if you can recreate the same mental and emotional patterns. You'll find lots of ideas and suggestions for doing this in later chapters.

We all need role models. Modelling is one of the keys to accelerated learning. If you model effectively, you can take giant steps forward and save yourself months, perhaps years, of effort by a little intelligent imitation. But don't forget – merely copying what someone else *does* will be relatively ineffective. The real secret is to find out what's going on in that powerhouse of human achievement, *the mind*, and generate it for yourself. The key to success will then be in your hands!

The Secret of Achieving Peak Performance

At the peak of tremendous and victorious effort, when the
blood is pounding in your head, all suddenly becomes
quiet within you. Everything seems clearer and brighter
than before, as if great spotlights have been turned on.
At that moment, you have the conviction you
contain all the power in the world. There is no
more precious moment in life than this, and you will
work very hard for years just to taste it again.

Yuriy Vlasov, weightlifter

In November 1993, the England rugby team took to the field against New Zealand at Twickenham. Few gave them a chance. The mighty All Blacks had trounced every team they'd played on the tour and acquired a reputation for being humourless, brutal and totally ruthless.

Once the match had started, though, it soon became obvious that the England players had other ideas. The forwards harried and chased. The backs played like men possessed. The crowd, at first subdued, began to get behind their team. The more they cheered, the better the English team performed. The better they played, the more supportive became the crowd. Against all the odds, England won the match 15–9.

What happened that day? How were the English players able to confound all expectations? Was it simply that they played above themselves and caught the All Blacks on an off-day? Perhaps. It certainly couldn't have happened if they hadn't been at their absolute best. Every sports person knows that there are days when you get 'on a high', when everything goes your way and you feel as if you can't go wrong. And other days where you just can't get it right. The England players discovered this for themselves soon after their memorable victory against the All Blacks when they struggled narrowly to beat an unfancied Scotland side and then went on to slump to defeat against the Irish.

Bob Willis, the fast bowler, had such a glory day against the Australians in

1981, when he took seven wickets and brought victory to an England cricket team that was seemingly heading for defeat. Have you ever experienced that unbeatable feeling? And the opposite, when everything you attempt seems to go wrong? Have you ever wondered why you feel and perform better on some days than others? Once you know why this happens, you can be at your best whenever you want. We'd like to share two very important clues with you.

Firstly, there *is* a special state of physical and mental alertness that leads to high-energy, positive attitudes, happiness and fun. You can only perform at your very best when you are feeling this way – but it is not a hit-and-miss affair. You can learn to achieve it whenever you want once you have the know-how.

The key to achieving peak performance is managing your emotional state. Winners continually experience positive emotions – such as enthusiasm, pleasure, commitment – and avoid the negatives – defeatism, boredom, depression, irritation, etc. Top sports stars know how to trigger the right feelings within themselves during the game. We cannot emphasize this enough.

The second important clue is this: successful sports people know that they will only perform well if they feel good *before* they begin. They realize that they won't be able to do their best unless they are already experiencing positive emotions at the start of the contest. Perhaps you've never thought of it like this before. Many people believe that feeling good is a result of playing well but, in fact, the reverse is true. Playing well and winning is the result of feeling good; being full of confidence and enjoying what you're doing; having the ability to concentrate fully; and feeling calm and relaxed, even under pressure.

One startling demonstration of this is the fire-walk. Our friend Richard attended a seminar given by a well-known personal development consultant who teaches his clients to walk over red-hot coals. Richard had been helping the organizers prepare the fire-beds and had not taken part in the 3-hour session which prepared the other participants for their experience. To his astonishment, and apprehension, the organizer asked him to lead the way.

'But I'm not prepared,' he argued. 'I missed the briefing.'

The organizer smiled. 'How would you stand if you were about to walk on fire?' he asked.

Richard changed his posture. 'Like this,' he replied.

'How would you move?'

Richard showed him.

'How would you walk?'

Richard thought for a moment.

'Then focus on your goals, repeat the phrase "cool, wet moss" and walk across. Go!'

Richard told us that the hot coals felt like a combination of popcorn and snow. And we know – in April 1994 we did it ourselves. 'What's this got to do with sport?' you may ask. The answer is simple. We were able to use the power of our minds to do the seemingly impossible without feeling any pain – not even a blister. Our friend was able to change his emotional state *in seconds* and do something most people think impossible. If he can do this and, as a consequence, reach the heights of physical achievement, then so can you.

You wouldn't want to be 'fired-up' all the time, though. You'd end up exhausted and overstressed. You need to balance periods of activity with recuperation time, to allow your mind and body to recover fully. Think about your car for a moment. If you left the headlights on overnight, your battery would go flat and you wouldn't be able to get the engine started in the morning. It's much the same with your energy levels. You must recharge your batteries or you will suffer from the adverse effects of stress and ill health, physically and emotionally. Top athletes like Linford Christie don't try to break the world record in every race because it's too exhausting. They plan their achievements over a whole season, thinking ahead to the really important event and aiming to peak at exactly the right moment.

We always advise our clients to make sure they balance the periods of intense physical training and competition with plenty of relaxation. All professional sports people are careful to do the same. For example, Steve Davis plays electronic games between snooker sessions, Jack Charlton goes fishing when he's not managing the Republic of Ireland football team, and many stars, including Nigel Mansell, Stephen Hendry and, in his day, Henry Cooper, play golf as a way of getting away from the pressures of their main sport.

Most professional players will have a nap in the afternoon on the day of an evening match. I don't think they'll be swimming or watching TV.

Steve Coppell (when asked what he and his fellow England players would be doing just before an important World Cup match)

Let's take a closer look at the connection between your mental and emotional state and your performance.

How your mental state influences your energy level

Energy is the most important ingredient in peak performance. You need to be able to mobilize as much of it as you can, which means experiencing positive attitudes and emotions. Take a few moments to study the table below.

Relationship between energy and emotion

	POSITIVE ATTITUDES AND EMOTIONS	NEGATIVE ATTITUDES AND EMOTIONS
HIGH ENERGY	Alert, inspired, full of energy Enthusiastic, passionate Confident, self-assured Calm, quiet mind **PEAK STATE**	Energetic, but tense, perhaps feeling threatened Not enjoyable, no fun Frustrated, overwhelmed by pressure Mind unsettled, desire to get even **ANGRY STATE**
LOW ENERGY	Calm, easy going, tension-free Leisurely, unfocussed, having fun Letting go and recovering Relaxed body, quiet mind **RESTING STATE**	Drained, listless, burnt out Bored, uninterested, mildly depressed, no fun Irritated, slightly tense Discouraged, disinterested **INCAPABLE STATE**

There is a strong connection between your emotional mood and your performance, and you can (and must) control it. You *can* take responsibility for your emotional state (we'll explain this in detail in Chapter 11). The first step is to be aware of which quadrant of the table you're in. Top sports people know this instinctively. They can get into *peak state* rapidly when they need to and drop into *resting state* immediately after a match.

You, too, should always try to stay on the positive, left-hand side of the table. When you are in peak state, you're at your absolute best but you wouldn't want to spend too much time there because you would eventually burn yourself out and fall into the bottom right-hand quadrant, the *incapable state*. You must spend plenty of time in the bottom left-hand, resting area, recharging your batteries. You need to go there frequently, consciously and deliberately, to de-stress and unwind.

Have you ever seen Wimbledon tennis stars being interviewed after a match? Within a few minutes of coming off court most of them are very composed, smiling and joking with the interviewer. How do they do it? With practice, it becomes as easy as turning off a television set and the more easily you can do it, the more energy you will have when you need it.

Now study the right-hand side of the table. Here are two quadrants you should try and avoid as much as possible. The *angry state* cell is a very dangerous one. You feel tense and bad-tempered. You know you're not at your best, which makes you frustrated. The more frustrated you feel, the more badly you perform until something snaps. Then you feel worse than ever. When you're in this state, the strain on your physical and emotional system is enormous. The temptation is to focus on what's going wrong, so you're painfully aware of the problems but have lost the ability to deal with the situation with a cool head.

The more time you spend in this angry state, the more energy you waste on unproductive activities and the more likely you are to go descending into the incapable state cell. Here, you have no energy and yet don't feel relaxed. It's hard to motivate yourself to get going again. Everything appears to be too much effort. This is the hardest quadrant to escape and, if you ever find yourself here during a match, it's a total disaster.

How good are you at managing your energy levels?

Spend a few moments thinking about the following questions.

When were you last in peak state? Was it morning, afternoon or evening? Is there a daily pattern to your energy swings? Is it related to what you have eaten or your sleep patterns? When you were last in peak state, how did it feel? What did you say to yourself? Close your eyes and imagine yourself back there now.

When were you last in resting state. How did you trigger resting state? How easy was it?

Are you able to anticipate when you are about to become angry? How do you normally cool down? When you do, do you go to resting state or incapable state? When you were last in angry state, did you want to get out of it or stay there?

When you face challenges, do you get nervous? Frightened? Angry? Intense? Or do you find yourself roused to new heights of endeavour?

Anchoring the peak performance state

Every experience you have ever had – good and bad – is filed in your memory banks where you can access it immediately should you want to. Your unconscious mind never forgets and, what's more, it doesn't just record events but also remembers how you felt at the time. What would you say if we told you that all the positive emotions you have experienced in the past are there to be used at will any time you want to feel at your best, instantly?

Well, you can use them, with a technique called *anchoring*. In essence, it's quite simple. Firstly you choose a trigger. This could be any gesture or code word(s) that you wouldn't normally use, such as '1, 2, 3, go, go, go', if you want to feel energized or '1,2,3, relax, relax', if you want to unwind. If the gesture or phrase is out of the ordinary, you will find it impossible to trigger the anchor by accident, for instance, relaxing when you want to feel fired-up, or vice versa.

David's 11-year-old son, Danny, has developed an anchor without realizing it. He uses it when he's playing football and often repeats it when he asks for (and receives!) a treat. He bends both arms up, clenches his fists and shouts 'yes' loudly. If he carries on in this way whenever he feels excited, by the time he reaches his teens it will have been reinforced so often he will be able to draw on it any time he likes. We suggest you try to develop and strengthen an anchor of your own for energizing yourself and another for relaxing.

Whenever you are in the desired state, reinforce your trigger. Let's say you are working on accessing the peak state at will. Whenever you are feeling this way, use the gesture or say the words, with as much emotional power as you can muster. With practice, the trigger and the feeling associated with it will become locked together in your nervous system, inseparable. It's exactly like Pavlov's dogs. You may remember that Pavlov rang a bell every time he fed the animals until, eventually, they would salivate at the sound of the bell alone, even though there was no food. Anchoring uses the same principle. In time, you will be able to execute your trigger and bring those empowering feelings flooding back.

If all this sounds a little far-fetched, consider the tennis player who bounces the ball repeatedly before serving, the batsman who prods the pitch between deliveries and the footballer who moves the ball fractionally to one side before taking a free kick. None of these actions is strictly necessary but they do help to focus concentration and bring about a state of calm. Otherwise, the player wouldn't feel quite right but probably wouldn't be able to say why. This is because the action acts as a trigger to reactivate feelings which have been anchored in the past.

The other way to install an anchor is to do it mentally when your mind and body are relaxed. We're going to cover this technique in much more detail in Chapter 12 (see page 95). It's good to know that there is a simple and effective way of feeling good any time you want! But, for now, we're going to turn to another matter that has a tremendous influence on your mood – the food you eat.

Nutrition for Winners

You are what you drink and I'm a bitter man.

The Macc Lads, rock group

Chris Wong was a third dan karate black belt who was suffering from such severe pain in his lower back that he was seeing Rex twice a week for treatment. It was only after several weeks that Rex enquired about his diet. It turned out that he was drinking at least 12 cups of coffee every day, each with three teaspoonsful of sugar. Rex didn't mince his words: he told him to stop immediately. A week later, the back pains had completely cleared.

How could drinking coffee with sugar have such a devastating effect on a fit young martial arts master? The answer is simple. Caffeine over-activates the adrenal glands, which control the sartorius muscles, which hold the pelvis in place. When these muscles are under stress, they cause the pelvis to twist, which results in pain in the lower back.

It's not only part-timers who can damage themselves. Many professionals are very strict about nutrition, and it's not only jockeys, coxes and feather-weight boxers. Take Ivan Lendl, the man who dominated men's tennis in the mid-1980s. At one time he was seen as a talented young man who just didn't have the bottle to break into the big time. It happened that a nutritionist who was watching him one day took him aside and asked him about his diet. Lendl admitted that he didn't give it much thought. He ate what he liked and didn't see how his play could be affected, but he was willing to try anything if there was a chance it would improve his results. The nutritionist changed his diet and, within a few weeks, Lendl had more energy and more stamina and, to his surprise, his on-court nerves had diminished too. To this day, he attributes his rise to the Number One slot to his change of diet.

If you still need convincing, let's give you one more example. A top American football team was plagued by injuries and struggling to win a match. The coach was approached by a group of holistic health practitioners who immediately placed all the players on a diet that eliminated sweet, over-refined, high-fat junk foods. The injury rate dropped dramatically and the team's results improved so much it reached the final of the prestigious Superbowl, the most important event in the American sporting calendar.

Unfortunately, the coach was persuaded to drop the services of the health practitioners before the final could be played. Their results soon deteriorated, the injury rate went back up to its previous level and they duly lost.

The world of nutrition seems bewildering at first. We're constantly bombarded with advice by the media – but beware: food companies are mainly interested in selling us their products rather than caring for our health. Take confectionery, for example. Manufacturers try to persuade us that their products give us energy because they contain lots of calories but they are actually being very economical with the truth. In fact, the energy gained from refined sugar products, although instant, is very short term. It peaks and then drops very quickly because of the effects on the blood-sugar level, which we'll explain shortly.

You'd be forgiven for thinking that the foods people most enjoy are usually bad for you and you'd be partly right. Many people take more care of their belongings than they do of their bodies. It reminds us of the car fanatic who took his pride and joy to the garage for a service, insisted that only the finest lubricants be used and, while he was waiting, had a hamburger and chips with cola, followed by ice cream, washed down with coffee!

Ten winning nutritional rules

We're going to cut through the confusion and give you ten basic guidelines to help you achieve peak performance through good nutrition. If you follow our advice, you'll be healthier, fitter and more emotionally stable. A healthy diet cleanses the body by helping it to get rid of the waste products which cause disease. It also reduces and can even prevent injuries. How many more reasons do you need for taking charge of your eating habits right now?

Ten winning nutritional rules

1   Balance alkaline- and acid-forming foods.

2   Reduce your fat and protein intake.

3   Don't mix starch and protein foods.

4   Eat only when you're hungry.

5   Avoid over-eating.

6   Eat small portions frequently.

7   Be careful what you drink and when.

8   Take vitamin and mineral supplements.

9   Shun all drugs.

10   Enjoy your food.

I Balance alkaline- and acid-forming foods

A healthy diet consists of approximately 80 per cent alkaline-forming and 20 per cent acid-forming foods. It's not that alkaline-forming foods are good and acid-forming foods are bad, it's achieving the right balance that's important. Alkaline-forming foods include virtually all fruits and vegetables, most nuts and millet. All other foods are acid-forming, including flesh foods, sugary foods, grains (except millet) and dairy products. Please understand that we're talking about the effect the food has on the stomach during and after digestion, not its chemical composition. For example, citrus fruits are chemically acidic but alkaline-forming once they reach the digestive system.

As you may have noticed, the alkaline-forming foods are all grown in the soil and most are ripened by the sun. We are convinced, after many years of study and helping thousands of patients to recover from illness and achieve good health, that the healthiest diet is vegetarian. Vegetarians have more stamina, energy, resilience and strength than flesh-eaters and are less prone to injury. Research has consistently shown this to be true. You'll also notice that the foods we're recommending have a high water content, which means you won't feel as thirsty as you did before and can cut down on your liquid intake.

The best proof is, of course, results and here the evidence is overwhelming. Among the world-class athletes following a vegetarian regime are:

- Martina Navratilova, the greatest female tennis player of all time
- David Scott, the only man to win the Iron Man Triathlon six times
- Ed Moses, undefeated 400-metres hurdles champion
- Murray Rose, freestyle swimming world-record holder
- Bill Pickering, English Channel swimming world-record holder
- Carl Lewis, multi-Olympic medallist and world-record holder

The key to good health and vitality is to avoid all dead, decaying, processed, poisoned (by chemical additives) and refined foods. Use fresh foods wherever possible and, if you feel you can't live without meat, choose white meats (such as hand-reared poultry) or fish, which contain less fat. Eat mainly natural, whole, living foods. The strongest and fittest creatures in the natural world do – ask any elephant, giraffe, bull or horse. They'll heartily recommend it!

I don't eat any meat, wheat or dairy products. When you're used to clean, fresh flavours anything else tastes disgusting.

Katherine Monbiot, international arm wrestler

2 Reduce your fat and protein intake

One of the biggest misconceptions is that the higher your protein intake, the better. Certainly a little protein and fat help to keep your body in good working order but you don't need as much as some would have you believe. A daily intake of 30–40 grams (1–1½ ounces) of protein is quite sufficient for most people. Protein does build muscle but most people, including the vast majority of sports people, get quite enough as part of their normal diet. Too much causes excess acidity, injuries to joints, arthritis and ultimately decalcification of the bones.

Muscle building requires a strength and endurance exercise programme and sufficient carbohydrate, not protein, and you'll certainly get enough in the nutritional plan we're suggesting.

Ideally, 60 per cent of the diet should be fresh fruit and vegetables, preferably eaten raw. Another 20 per cent should be grains, leaving 10 per cent fats and 10 per cent protein. Some nutritionists would even say that 10 per cent protein is too high. After all, human breast milk contains only 2½ per cent. Don't be taken in by the glossy marketing of the food processors; they have a vested interest in persuading you to eat more meat and dairy foods than you need.

Did you know that there is more usable protein in a large baked potato than in half a kilogram (1 pound) of steak? Remember, we said *usable* protein. It's not the protein which you eat that matters but the protein which your body is able to assimilate. Vegetable protein is absorbed more readily than protein from flesh foods. It's a common misconception that protein is missing from plant foods: many vegetables (including potatoes, onions and leafy green vegetables) actually do contain complete protein.

Whatever your previous beliefs about protein, we're sure it won't come as a big surprise to you that we recommend reducing your consumption of fat. People who exercise vigorously can cause themselves serious injury, and even death, if they eat too much fat. It clogs the arteries, which imposes extra strain on the heart. We know of a man in his 40s, who had eaten a typical Western diet for many years, who took up jogging. He went out one morning for a run and never returned. He was found dead of a heart attack less than half a kilometre (400 yards) from his home.

Carbohydrate helps you to exercise longer and harder and stave off exhaustion. It is vitally important if you take part in endurance events, such as marathon running or cycling. Nor do you have to buy those expensive branded supplement foods advertized in sports magazines. If you have a well-balanced diet, along the lines we suggest, everyday foods such as bananas are just as beneficial.

For example, Nathan Pritikin was a health expert who ran a longevity study centre in California, USA, and had a reputation for bringing very ill people back to full health. All his clients were placed on a diet which was high in complex carbohydrates and low in protein and fat. To demonstrate the effectiveness of the diet, he worked with a group of runners competing in a 160-kilometre (100-mile) race. They weren't even allowed vitamin and mineral supplements. Needless to say, many so-called 'experts' were sceptical at first but they were forced to eat their words: three of Pritikin's runners came home in the first five.

We've found that the best way to alter your diet is to make small, gradual changes. Gradually cut back on the amounts of meat and dairy products. Like meat, dairy products are not necessary for good health; your body can't absorb high quantities efficiently. They are also high in fat and are mucous forming. As you reduce your meat and dairy-food intake, simultaneously increase your intake of complex carbohydrates – fruit, vegetables and whole grains – soon you will be feeling much better and enjoying your food more!

3 Don't mix starch and protein foods

Experiments carried out by Dr William Hay in the early years of this century revealed something very interesting: the digestive juices that process starches are different from those which assimilate proteins. When proteins and starches are eaten together, they fight in your stomach and take longer to digest.

To prevent this, avoid eating starchy foods and protein foods at the same meal. Avoid eating grains, potatoes and bananas with meat and dairy foods whenever possible. If you're thinking, 'That's impossible! How on earth can I do that?', we can assure you that it's really not that difficult. Just leave the potatoes and grains out of any meal that includes protein foods. It also helps if you eat fruit between meals, not with them.

If you lapse occasionally, don't worry. You can still enjoy the occasional pizza, baked potato with cheese, and apple pie if you want to, but try not to have them within 24 hours of an important match. We assure you, you'll soon feel the benefits.

Examples of starchy and protein foods

STARCHY FOODS	PROTEIN FOODS
Cereals and grains	Flesh foods
Refined sugar	Soya products
Bananas	Most dairy products
Pulses and legumes	
Potatoes	
Beer and lager	

4 Eat only when you're hungry

Are you surprised that we feel it necessary to advise you to eat only when you're hungry? Many people allow the clock to dictate when they should eat and often eat when they don't really want to, or force themselves to wait until mealtimes, by which time they're often ravenous and eat far more than their stomach can comfortably take.

Your body is a very sophisticated organism. Left to its own devices it will tell you if it needs feeding but, unfortunately, you've probably learned to ignore its messages. The chances are that you fit your eating patterns around work and other members of your family, which makes good sense socially but not from a nutritional point of view. Don't you think it's unlikely that everybody will need to eat at exactly the same time?

If you doubt what we're saying, try an experiment. Just for a week eat only when you're hungry and notice how much more energetic you feel.

5 Avoid over-eating

Take a look at the people around you. Few of us are as slim and trim as we could be. Because eating is a pleasurable pastime, most of us eat more than we need. At certain times of year, such as Christmas, we may feel obliged to eat far more than is good for us, which does nothing for our health and fitness – studies have shown that people who consistently under-eat are fitter and live longer than the rest of us.

Did you know that up to 80 per cent of your energy is taken up with digesting your food after eating? It's the reason people often feel sleepy after a heavy meal. Sports people have far better uses for this energy.

When you eat to excess, your body can't utilize the food readily and excess calories are turned into body fat, which nobody wants. Eat only enough for the energy you want to use. If you want to lose weight, do so gradually over a number of weeks. Don't feel that you have to clear your plate; there's no need to feel guilty.

6 Eat small portions frequently

Many top sports stars have adopted a regime known as *grazing*. It involves eating five or six times a day, which imposes less stress on the digestive system and helps to maintain the all-important blood-sugar level. Blood sugar is especially important because it determines your energy levels and has a direct impact on your emotional state. It works like this.

You must stabilize the amount of glucose in your bloodstream. As soon as it drops below a certain level, you find it hard to concentrate, become irritable and lose your drive. You're not even aware why your motivation has dropped and you probably couldn't really care: you're more interested in taking a nap.

When your blood cells are starved of glucose, your muscles become incapable of doing what you want them to.

When we use the term *blood sugar*, we're not talking of the processed sugar that many people put in their hot drinks and eat in cakes and confectionery. These refined sugary foods cause a blood-sugar *spike*. The blood-sugar level rises quickly, making you feel good for a while, then drops down just as quickly, leaving you feeling drained.

Natural sugar from complex carbohydrates is not absorbed as quickly as this but it is available for a longer period. To keep your blood-sugar level high on a consistent basis, we suggest that you eat small meals and snacks five or six times a day. Never miss breakfast – your body needs the nutrients and sugars it provides – but avoid large breakfasts. It is better to have something easily digestible, such as fruit, since a large meal too early in the day takes longer to digest and hampers the elimination process. Have a piece of fruit or a wholegrain snack at mid-morning and mid-afternoon and a more substantial lunch or evening meal. Our recommended pattern is set out in the table below.

Recommended eating pattern

TIME OF DAY	FOOD
Breakfast	Fruit OR wholegrain cereal / toast
Mid-morning	Fruit OR wholegrain snack
Lunch	Large salad with baked potato OR hearty vegetable soup with whole grain snack
Mid-afternoon	Fruit OR wholegrain snack
Evening	White meat / Fish with vegetables OR Vegetarian main course OR Jacket potatoes / Brown rice with vegetables

You'll have noticed that whole grains play a large part in our nutritional plan. There are many to choose from – brown rice, millet, barley, oats, buckweat, etc., and wheat. But too much wheat, even wholemeal, is not advisable, since it clogs your digestive system. The equivalent of four slices of bread per day is quite sufficient.

One more tip about large meals: your digestive system doesn't function very efficiently when you're under strain, so avoid eating large meals when you're feeling tired, stressed or over-excited. The best time to eat is when you're in the resting state (see page 39).

7 Be careful what you drink and when

The ideal drink is pure, fresh, spring water. Herb teas and diluted fresh fruit juice are also very beneficial. But what do most Westerners drink? Coffee, tea, fizzy drinks and alcohol account for the bulk of liquids consumed. All of these stress the body in one way or another and leave you less able to perform at your best. We strongly recommend that you avoid caffeine at all times; it interferes with the absorption of iron and other minerals from food. Herbal tea and cereal coffee are good alternatives, and coffee that has been decaffeinated using a water-based process.

As for alcohol, it makes sense to avoid it altogether up to 24 hours before you take part in sport and never to drink more than 2 or 3 half litres or pints of beer or lager, or 4 or 5 measures of spirits or glasses of wine, at a time. Also, confine your alcohol drinking to two or three sessions a week at most.

Now think about *when* you should drink. The sensible answer is, of course, when you're thirsty! Yet how many of us drink for the sake of it, whether we need it or not? Never drink with meals. Liquids dilute your digestive juices, so the vitamins, minerals and energy are not available to you as quickly, the very last thing that an active person needs.

8 Take vitamin and mineral supplements

If you're exercising a great deal, you may be losing more vitamins and minerals than you take in, which could have disastrous effects on your health in the long term. In addition, eating a poor diet, combining foods incorrectly and drinking with meals causes poor assimilation of nutrients into the body, while modern farming practices reduce the nutritional value of the food. Over-cooking, too, destroys vitamins and minerals, as well as robbing the food of its flavour. What should you do to redress the balance?

The answer is to take supplements – not the branded sort, advertized in sports magazines, which promise bigger muscles, more energy and less pain – but the natural vitamin and mineral tablets available from all good health food shops. Take one multi-vitamin tablet and at least 500 milligrams of vitamin C every day. These supplements are relatively inexpensive and ensure that you have sufficient vitamins and minerals to provide a buffer between you and nutrient deficiency.

Also make sure you have sufficient magnesium: athletes have died from a magnesium deficiency due to excessive exercise. Don't let it happen to you!

One final word on the expensive, branded sports foods you see in sports shops and magazines: don't be taken in. The manufacturers will seek to baffle you with science but the fact is that there is no magic wand and no substitute for a balanced diet and lots of the right sort of training.

9 Shun all drugs

The use of non-medicinal drugs is extremely dangerous. The short-term benefits are more than outweighed by the long-term side-effects, such as skin blemishes, blubber where muscle used to be and the ultimate collapse of your vital organs. Drugs, including artificial growth hormones, are not even worth giving a second thought. We're not moralizing here; if you want to cheat, it's between you and your conscience. We're simply giving you the facts from a health and fitness point of view.

We're not just talking about the so-called performance-enhancing drugs. Most of us are aware of the havoc wreaked by those two highly addictive substances, nicotine and alcohol. Cigarette smoking is harmful no matter how fit you are. It inhibits lung capacity and reduces the oxygen supply. It also narrows the arteries leading to the heart, which reduces the blood supply just when it is needed the most – during peak performance – and can cause heart damage and even death.

10 Enjoy your food

By now, you're probably thinking we're a couple of kill-joys who don't like you to enjoy your food. Nothing could be further from the truth! We enjoy our food as much as anyone but the problem is to balance titillating the taste buds against the long-term drawbacks – lower energy, poor performance and unnecessary health problems. Health and fitness are not the same but they are closely related and you won't enjoy either unless you eat wisely.

If you are tempted to eat something you know you shouldn't, stop for a moment. Consider the problems you may be storing up for yourself in the future. Think about the pain of losing an event you should have won because you couldn't summon up enough energy, strength or composure when you needed it. And then dismiss the idea of eating the offending substance from your mind.

Finally, a few words of reassurance. Occasionally breaking the rules won't really harm you but make sure that at least 90 per cent of your diet is healthy, which allows for a little indulgence from time to time. Eating a small piece of chocolate every once in a while won't damage your health but eating it every day would, so be sensible. Eat well, enjoy your food and take a pride in your achievements, both on and off the sports field.

Let's Get Physical

When you exercise, you start to discover the individual within yourself. You go through the concentration, patience and joyful discipline of becoming that individual. The struggle is for the prize that is yourself.

George Sheehan, American doctor and writer, known as 'the Running Doctor'

He was facing one of the biggest challenges of his life, a gruelling contest, one against one, that would achieve his ambition – the World Championship. His research had revealed that, on the rare occasions when his Soviet opponent had lost, it was because he had faded in the later stages of the game. He didn't seem to have enough stamina to see a long match through to the bitter end. This made his mind up. For the next 6 months, he would put himself through a punishing 3-hour work-out every day. He would swim underwater laps to build up his lung power, play tennis, run and do aerobic exercises. His coaches thought he'd gone crazy. They advised him to concentrate on his technique but he ignored them.

What sport do you think he was engaged in? Boxing? Tennis? No. It was *chess*. We're talking about Bobby Fisher, who met Boris Spassky for the World Chess Championship in 1972. Fisher's advisors had noticed that Spassky's posture was poor and was almost certainly hampering his lung capacity and cutting off the oxygen supply to his brain, explaining the tiredness. Fisher turned out to be absolutely right. Spassky did indeed lose because he made silly mistakes in the later stages of key games. Fisher's rigorous routine had paid off.

You, as a sports enthusiast, already know that there is no substitute for stamina and fitness, whatever you're doing. The business community increasingly appreciate this, which is why many companies are now building gymnasia for their employees and allowing them time during the working day to use them. They know that there are many benefits of regular exercise. Here are some of the main ones:

- Effective weight control
- Greater self-confidence

- Better clarity of thought
- More enthusiasm
- Higher energy levels, more vitality
- More stable, happier emotions
- Increased endurance and stamina
- Better concentration and memory
- Increased resistance to disease
- Better digestion
- Deeper, more satisfying sleep
- Lower stress levels
- Reversing of the ageing process

The last point may well surprise you but it's been well researched and proven time and time again. Dr George Sheehan, for example, is well known in the USA as 'the Running Doctor'. He took up running at the age of 45 years and was still at it a quarter of a century later. Now approaching 70, he continues to run marathons and looks like a man in his 40s – fit, slim and full of vibrant energy.

Fatigue makes cowards of us all.

Vince Lombardi, American football coach (1913–70)

Exercise is highly addictive; once you've tasted its benefits, you'll never want to lose them. Both mind and body work better when the body is fit. What's more, physical activity and the emotions are closely connected, because it causes hormones called *endorphins* to be released into the blood-stream. These 'happy hormones' are released after 5 or 10 minutes' exercise and their effect can still be felt several hours later. Moreover, anyone can exercise. Do you recall Chris Brogan, the paraplegic athlete featured in Chapter 2? He does a 40-kilometre (25-mile) 'push' every Sunday, whatever the weather, 27 kilometres (17 miles) every other week-day and works out regularly in a gym.

In this chapter, we're going to discuss aerobic and anaerobic exercise, the basic rules of exercising, warming up and the vital importance of loosening and stretching the muscles every day, correct breathing and recovering from injury. However, we won't attempt to suggest a specific exercise programme since this must be tailored to suit your individual requirements and to the sports that you play.

Aerobic and anaerobic exercise

Exercise can either be aerobic or anaerobic. *Aerobic* means 'in combination with oxygen'. In other words, it is exercise you can do comfortably without having to gasp for breath. Aerobic exercise builds stamina and burns fat, just what sportsmen and women need.

Anaerobic literally means 'in the absence of oxygen'. This includes any exercise which involves intense, short bursts of energy that leave you breathless, such as tennis, weightlifting and sprinting. Anaerobic exercise burns starch and builds strength.

Most types of exercise can be either or both, depending on how concentrated it is. Walking, swimming, jogging and ice skating are aerobic provided that they are engaged in gently, over a period of time, so that the heartbeat remains fairly steady. But they can also be anaerobic if they are hurried or done to excess so that the heartbeat is racing, as occurs during moments of intense effort. Too much anaerobic exercise uses up the body's supply of carbohydrate. Once this happens, you start to run down your blood-sugar level, and you already know what this means – you lose energy, perhaps even feel faint, and you crave food.

All training programmes should begin with aerobics until lung capacity is increased. Then, and only then, should you move on to anaerobic exercise, perhaps 3 to 6 months after starting your regime. If you think you can stay fit by playing an aggressive game of squash once a week and little else, think again. You could easily end up with torn muscles or, worse, a heart attack.

Expanding your aerobic capacity improves your ability to ingest and utilize oxygen (the source of vibrant energy and good health). Achieve this and you will burn off excess fat, increase your energy, reduce your stress levels, strengthen your immune system and sustain fewer injuries.

Obviously, while you're exercising, you need to know whether you've moved beyond aerobic exercise into anaerobic. Fortunately, there's a simple test for this:

- Is your breathing steady – or laboured?
- Is the activity stressful – or not?
- Can you still hold a conversation – or are you too short of breath?
- Can you keep going for 15–20 minutes – or do you feel exhausted?

If you can answer 'yes' to the *first part* of all these questions, you're in the aerobic zone.

The basic rules of exercising

How should you go about designing a training programme for yourself? Well, first, a few words of warning. It is wise to consult your doctor and perhaps have a full medical check-up, especially if you haven't exercised regularly for a few years. Although exercise is fun, it's also hard work. You deliberately put extra stress on your body in order to increase its resistance to additional physical exertion. You challenge the muscular and aerobic systems, increase your heart rate and activate the sweat glands.

The next two questions to ask yourself are 'How often?' and 'How intense?'

Ideally you should build up to 20–30 minutes aerobic exercise three or four times a week. Don't allow yourself to be tempted to miss a few sessions here and there – this would be like taking two steps forward and one back. Find activities that you enjoy and seek variety; there are plenty to choose from – running, swimming, cycling, rowing, aerobic dancing, etc. If you want to, join a gym or an exercise club, then you can enjoy your exercise with like-minded people and perhaps make new friends.

The best and most easily measured indication of the intensity of exercise is your heart rate. You must be very careful here. Your maximum target heart rate for aerobic exercise should be 220 beats per minute minus your age so, if you are 20 years old, your target is 200 beats per minute. If you're 50, your target is 170. Don't overdo it. If you feel stressed or tired, ease off.

Schedule your exercise into a time that suits you. You don't have to get up early to go for a run before breakfast unless you particularly want to. In fact, the best time is in the afternoon when your body is already warmed up and active.

Only when you can hold your target heart rate for 20 minutes or so without discomfort should you attempt anaerobic exercise, and then little by little, until your body is safely used to it.

Why not buy yourself a small notebook and use it as a training log? You can write out your training plan and compare your progress with your targets.

Our basic rules of exercising are designed for enthusiastic amateurs who want to achieve a higer level of fitness than before. However, if you are, or aspire to be, a professional athlete, your training requirements will go beyond what we've described here and we would advise you to seek help from a qualified coach, if you haven't already done so.

Warming up – the importance of loosening and stretching exercises

Warming up is a must. If you're properly warmed up, you'll perform far more efficiently right from kick-off and be less likely to injure yourself. For instance, the main reason hamstrings get torn is because the player hasn't fully warmed up. The more time you spend stretching your muscles and mobilizing your joints, the better.

If your sport involves long periods of standing fairly still followed by sudden and rapid movement (such as fielding in cricket or baseball), stretching and mobilizing exercises are even more important.

We've designed a 'bio-energetic' routine which can be used at any time. It's worth doing some of these exercises during the day, especially if you're feeling tense or stressed. They will help you to feel more relaxed and in control. Read them on to a cassette tape and listen as you do them. They improve muscle flexibility and joint mobility, help avoid muscular and joint problems, such as arthritis and rheumatism, and improve health on all levels.

All mobilizing exercises should be practised with the correct breathing, so keep your breathing even and rhythmic (this allows the joints to move more freely).

When you exercise, concentrate on what you're doing. Focus your attention on it and mentally direct your breath towards the area you are working on. Breathe *out* as you're stretching and *in* as you relax. This helps you to stretch further without imposing extra strain on the muscles.

Bio-energetic exercises for stretching and loosening

Repeat each of the following several times to thoroughly stretch and loosen the body.

Neck

Rotate the neck gently in a semi-circle. Never turn it in a full circle or force it backwards as this stresses the facet joints. Gently ease the left ear towards the left shoulder and the right ear towards the right shoulder. Move the head down and up, as if nodding.

Shoulders

Rotate the shoulders gently in both directions. Raise and lower them, as if shrugging.

Arms

Swing your arms in big circles, backwards and forwards. Then, to expand the chest, bend your arms, raise to shoulder level, elbows out and fists together, then swing them back horizontally as far as you can.

Hands

Shake the hands. Rotate the wrists and then stretch your fingers by pushing the splayed fingers of both hands together.

Trunk

To loosen the trunk thoroughly:

● Bend the whole body backwards, forwards and side to side to loosen the back. Twist to the left and right, keeping the pelvis still. Rotate the trunk clockwise and anti-clockwise, remembering to keep the back straight.

● Sit on the floor. Place the soles of your feet together and push your knees to the floor. Now bend forwards until your head is as close to the floor as possible without bending your back.

● Still sitting, open your legs sideways as far as possible, extend your arms forwards and bend your body forwards to touch the floor. Alternate this with gently lowering your chest to your right leg, then the left leg, and so on.

● Still on the floor, stretch both legs in front of you. Bend your body forward and grab your feet without bending the knees. Again, keep the back straight. (Note: Do not do this exercise if pregnant.)

● Sit on your heels with your back straight. Lean backwards as far as you can, holding your ankles and keeping your knees as close together as possible.

Legs

Repeat each of the following exercises with the right leg.

● Place your left heel on a table or chair and, keeping your legs straight, bend forward to stretch the hamstring.

● Bend your left knee and lean to the left, stretching your right leg. This stretches the quadriceps (the large muscle that supports the knee) of the left leg, while stretching the thigh muscles of the right. Repeat, leaning to the right.

Correct breathing

Have you ever paid any attention to your breathing? After all, it's an activity you quite happily leave to your unconscious mind most of the time. Did you know that you could survive for several weeks without food, and a few days without water, but less than 5 minutes without oxygen?

Oxygen is vital for stamina and energy, and influences your emotional state. Try this for yourself. Breathe slowly and heavily for 2 minutes and notice how you feel. When you deepen and slow your breathing, your emotions quieten down. Control your breathing and you control your emotions; control your emotions and your breathing changes. Yes, it's true. All breathing has an equivalent emotional rhythm and it's a two-way process. So, if you want to experience positive emotions, you *must* breathe correctly.

Unfortunately, most of us don't breathe anything like as deeply as we should. When our breathing is too shallow, only the air in the top half of the lung is changed, leaving stale air in the lower part, where it can cause lethargy and even illness. Deep breathing clears the stale air out of the system and helps us to absorb pure, fresh oxygen. That's why it's important to learn to use the full capacity of the lungs until it becomes a natural and habitual way of breathing.

Deep breathing increases your chances of winning. For example, listen to the top tennis players as they serve. Jimmy Connors was known for his loud grunt. Monica Seles and André Agassi, among others, make a loud 'aaaah' sound every time they hit the ball. They've often been accused of doing this to put their opponents off but, even if this were true, it's not the main reason. The grunt is a sudden and very pronounced exhalation, which prepares the lung for a deep inhalation, helps muscles to relax and helps to keep the concentration focussed.

We're offering four breathing exercises which help you to breathe more deeply, increase your lung capacity and stimulate your nervous system. If you prefer, you can do them in time to slow, rhythmic music. It helps if you are reasonably relaxed before you start, so if you have just finished physical activity, wait a few minutes. Don't overdo it – if you start to feel dizzy or faint, stop at once.

1   The complete breath

Inhale through the nose, right into the pit of the stomach, expanding the ribs and stomach outwards, filling the entire lung. Hold for 4 seconds. Then breathe out through the mouth by contracting the stomach, expelling all the air, as if squeezing all the air out of a balloon. Repeat several times with a continuous, flowing action. The complete breath gets much more oxygen into the lung.

2   Rhythmic breathing

Breathe in through the nose for 4 seconds, hold for 4, then exhale for 4. Gradually increase the count until you can breathe in for, say, a count of 15. The longer the exhalation, the better. Rhythmic breathing vitalizes the body, increases your energy and alters your emotional state. You can easily do it while walking and it's especially beneficial if you are out in the country or by the sea.

3   The cleansing breath

Inhale fully, then purse your lips tightly and force the air out as hard as you can. As you breathe out, bend further and further forward until every last ounce of air is expelled. Then repeat. This expels all the stale air from the bottom half of the lungs and helps to revitalize you, so do it especially when you feel lethargic.

4   The nerve-strengthening breath

Stand erect. Inhale and retain a complete breath, and extend both arms out in front of you. Then slowly draw the hands back towards the shoulders, tightly clenching the fists as you do so. Then rapidly push the fists away, draw them back towards you, push them away, draw them back, and repeat five or six times. Finally, exhale vigorously through the mouth. Repeat several times. This stimulates the nervous system and develops energy and vitality.

Recovering from injury

Many great sporting personalities – including Greg Lemond and Thomas Muster – have returned from serious injury and achieved even greater success than before. You can do the same if you have a basic understanding of how the body heals itself and the part played by the mind.

It may seem hard to believe but most people who get injured at sport, even full contact sports, actually inflict the injury on themselves. Pulled muscles, sprains and strains are self-induced. The most common are knee and ankle injuries but it is strained calf muscles and hamstrings that take longest to heal. Do you realize that you can get back into action far more quickly if you break a bone than if you damage a joint or strain or tear a ligament (although we wouldn't wish either on you). A sensible routine, which includes warming up before and warming down after exercise, reduces the risk of injury considerably.

Most injuries heal of their own accord but you can speed up the rate of progress with just a little know-how. For instance, as soon as you injure a joint or muscle, apply an icepack. You can use a bag of frozen peas, which easily moulds around the injured area, to reduce the inflammation, unless the muscles are in spasm. If they are, you need heat, such as a hot-water bottle or a hot bath.

It is always wise to see your doctor just in case the injury is more serious than you thought. He or she should check the damage carefully and recommend suitable treatment, such as physiotherapy. Often, doctors prescribe drugs, such as steroids, to speed recovery but there are other approaches too, such as osteopathy, chiropractic and acupuncture. Together with homoeopathic and herbal remedies, these therapies, in the hands of a competent practitioner, accelerate the healing process. Common herbal remedies include arnica cream for sprains, strains and bruising, calendula for open wounds and comfrey (symphytum) for broken bones. Using natural remedies will not necessarily kill the pain but it will promote rapid healing with complete safety.

With all injuries, a combination of rest and gentle exercise is advisable. Providing your doctor agrees, it is wise to exercise as soon as possible after the injury. Use the gentle stretching and mobilizing exercises we suggest, putting the damaged part through its full range of movements, as long as it's not too painful. As you do this, mentally direct your breath towards the area. Mentally sending healing energy to the injured part greatly speeds up recovery. Our nutritional guidelines will also help you to recover more quickly.

If you're determined to make a rapid recovery, you can also call on the power of your mind to assist you. This is best done when your body is relaxed, which we explain in detail in Chapter 10. Imagine the affected area healing itself, direct your breath and your healing energies towards it and see the joint or muscle being healed in your mind's eye. Finally, visualize yourself back in action, performing at your best once again. This is the essence of the hypno-healing technique which David has used successfully for a wide range of physical ailments, from minor aches and pains to arthritis.

Speeding up your recovery

Studies of athletes who made a complete recovery from serious injury revealed that they had the following characteristics in common:

- They were totally dedicated to regaining full health. Most had committed themselves to getting in even better shape than before.

- They approached rehabilitation one step at a time and refused to be impatient or discouraged.

- They were fully involved in the healing process. They accepted responsibility for their own progress and participated in the treatment. For example, doing the exercises and visualizations made them feel as if they were influencing what was taking place.

- They focussed on their own progress rather than comparing themselves with others. They concentrated on what they could do that they couldn't previously.

In this chapter, we've offered you some simple guidelines for exercising, breathing and recovering from injury. If you follow them, you'll be in good shape and have fewer injuries. You'll be more energetic and in a more positive frame of mind. You'll have laid very firm foundations for becoming a winner!

Taking Charge of Your Attitudes and Beliefs

You create your own reality with your thoughts, feelings and attitudes.

Dynamic Living Principle No. 1

In the 1993 Ladies' Singles final at Wimbledon, Jana Novotna held a commanding lead over her opponent, Steffi Graf, in the final set, yet lost the match. Why?

In the summer of the same year, the USA soccer team beat England in a four-nation tournament. The English players were physically fit, technically superior and more experienced. How on earth could they lose?

In 1989, Mike Tyson, the undisputed World Heavyweight Boxing Champion, lost his crown to the rank outsider James 'Buster' Douglas. Until then, Tyson had been unbeaten and regarded as the finest fighter for a generation. What went wrong?

The answer can be summed up in two words: *attitude* and *belief*. Whatever your activity, you will only excel if you have the right attitude and believe that you can do so. This is undoubtedly the key to performing well consistently, under pressure.

Whatever happens to you in life is not nearly as important as your attitude towards it. Events and situations, good or bad, will only affect you if you choose to let them to do so. This is driven home very quickly in sport. If you're a boxer, for instance, a few blows to the face make the point in an instant.

Your beliefs govern your success. Let's imagine a golfer who consistently scores in the high 80s; he believes himself to be a 'high 80s' sort of player. One day, he's on form and scores a fantastic 36 on the first nine holes. What goes through his mind? 'I'm playing above myself today. It's not like me.' So, at least unconsciously, he adjusts, makes silly mistakes, misses easy putts and hits the bunkers. He plays the last nine holes in 48, to give himself a total score of 84. If he'd have carried on playing as well as he did in the first half, he'd have ended up with 72. His performance has fallen in line with his beliefs.

Self-deprecating beliefs and attitudes are the kiss of death to any athlete. They leave a solo performer with virtually no chance of winning and are equally damaging in team sports, since just one person with a poor attitude can harm morale. The person with the attitude problem is the weakest link in the chain, just waiting to be exploited by the opposition.

How does this happen? Well, first of all, you're not in the right mental or emotional state to perform at your best. Next, it reduces your energy level, your strength and your stamina, because emotions directly affect the physiology and biochemistry of the body. Finally, it undermines team spirit. The point is very clear. You must programme negative attitudes and beliefs out of your life if you want to succeed at sport, or at anything else.

> *You really have got to want to win and believe you can win. If you get into the ring thinking you will lose, you already have. If you can knock out your negative thoughts, you've already won half the battle.*
>
> Frank Bruno, British heavyweight boxer

The word 'attitude' is much bandied about but what exactly is it? Quite simply, it is the outward expression of an underlying thought or feeling. If you're thinking happy thoughts, you'll have a happy attitude. But if you're thinking 'I can't do it', you'll have a defeatist attitude. Obvious, isn't it?

Attitudes, thoughts and feelings are closely connected to your beliefs, so it's worth taking some time to understand where these beliefs come from. Knowledge you have gained, the people around you, and your environment can all influence your beliefs. What you have achieved in the past is also very important. If you once attempted something and succeeded, you'll believe that it's possible to do it again. If you tried and failed, you're likely to think it's beyond your capabilities.

The biggest misconception that many people hold on to is that their beliefs are somehow ingrained into them, fixed and impossible to change. Nothing could be further from the truth. All your beliefs have been learned. When you were born, your mind was a blank slate; you had no beliefs of your own. As you grew, you were exposed to the beliefs of the people around you and you could accept or reject what you were told. Of course, you may have decided it was better to go along with your parents than argue against them, even if, in your heart, you didn't agree. Perhaps you were even punished for holding beliefs they didn't share. The shaping of a child's beliefs is called *conditioning*.

Since you learned your beliefs, and anything that is learned can be un-learned, it follows that you can consciously and deliberately alter your beliefs if you want to. Most people, often unknowingly, do it all the time. And if you can change your beliefs, you can consciously change your attitudes.

If that sounds difficult, just think about it for a moment. When Dr Roger Bannister decided to attempt to run a mile in under 4 minutes, the 'experts' thought he had gone mad. Many had tried and failed (the closest anyone had come was 4 minutes 1.4 seconds in 1945) and the 4-minute mile was believed to be beyond the realms of human capability.

But Bannister was convinced that the 4-minute barrier was only mental, and he was determined to prove it. Because he didn't want anyone to try to talk him out of it, he trained alone so as not to be influenced by coaches steeped in the conventional wisdom. On 6 May 1954, on a chilly, windy day in Oxford, paced by two friends, he clocked 3 minutes 59.4 seconds, knocking 2 full seconds off the old record. He'd done it!

Than an amazing thing happened. No less than 37 other athletes broke the 4-minute barrier during the following year; within 2 years, over 300 had done it. The previously 'impossible' 4-minute mile had come within the reach of many athletes. What had occurred to make the impossible possible? They'd changed their beliefs! Suddenly, hundreds of athletes *believed* they could do what they'd previously thought they could not. They had adopted a different attitude towards the 4-minute mile.

Take a piece of paper and a pen and spend a few moments now writing down the beliefs which you will need to achieve your goals, positive beliefs that will drive you forward. Start with 'I have the ability', 'I deserve to succeed', and 'I am as good as anyone else'. Remember, reading through the exercises won't help you very much, but doing them will!

Empowering attitudes

We've selected ten attitudes which, if you adopt them as your own, will help you to achieve better results consistently. We're not saying that our list includes all the positive attitudes you need; you may wish to add a few more of your own and may even disagree with some of ours. But whatever your list, simply giving it some thought will help you to focus your attention on the empowering attitudes you need to adopt.

Ten empowering attitudes for a winner

1 I have a positive mental attitude.

2 I can do it.

3 I accept responsibility for myself and my performance.

4   I'm in competition with myself.

5   I live in the present moment.

6   I am fearless, bold and courageous.

7   I deserve to be successful.

8   Failure is not defeat.

9   I shall persist until I succeed.

10   I enjoy what I'm doing.

1   I have a positive mental attitude

'I automatically focus on the positive. I am positive about life. I am influenced only by positive thoughts and positive people. I think, talk and act positively at all times.'

It can be quite a challenge to be positive all the time, especially when you're taking your first tentative steps. Other people often seem to dwell on the down side of every situation. Your aim is to follow the example of the second man in the following poem:

> *Two men looked through prison bars,*
> *One saw mud and the other saw stars.*

Imagine what would happen if you surrounded yourself with negative people. Perhaps you already do. If so, do their defeatist attitudes sap your self-belief and determination? If so, it's important to learn to ignore them, even if it means spending less time in their company and even gently easing them out of your life.

One man who was always positive was Jimmy Connors. Towards the end of his career, he had just reached the semi-finals of the US Open Tennis Championships when he was amazed to hear that the reigning champion had expressed relief at being eliminated in an early round. He'd apparently had a heavy schedule and felt he needed a rest. Thirty-eight year-old Connors was heard to exclaim, in total disbelief: 'How on earth can anybody actually *want* to lose?'

2   I can do it

'I'm equal to any challenge. I have faith in myself. I have confidence in my abilities.'

You need to develop a mentally tough approach, born of quiet self-assurance but not complacency. This doesn't mean shouting your mouth off to others (people who do this are usually covering up a *lack* of confidence).

Your level of self-esteem places a ceiling on your potential since low self-esteem can only lead to low achievement. If you have a poor self-image, it's very important that you spend time building up your self-confidence. Follow the advice in our book, *Creating Confidence – the Secrets of Self-Esteem*. Not only will you feel better about yourself, you'll project a winning aura to your opponents too!

3 I accept responsibility for myself and my performance

'Success is not a matter of luck. I will do the very best I can without blaming others if I don't do as well as I would like. I am in control of my own destiny.'

This attitude puts the onus on *you*, and that's exactly where it should be. What happens to people who blame the referee, the line judge, the weather or the crowd for their own failings? They lose! Your success depends entirely on you – your body, your mind, your attitude. Full stop.

> *You will not improve because you want to, you improve because you make it happen. You have got to find the ways to improve, make yourself a promise to improve and then actually carry it out.*

Steve Perryman, Tottenham Hotspur footballer

4 I'm in competition with myself

'I always give it my best shot. Every day, in every way, I'm getting better and better. I improve a little each day. I am good enough to win and I will.'

It is said that a thoroughbred racehorse never looks at the other horses, it just gallops as fast as it can. That's a very good attitude to hold because, as long as you do your best, you can always hold your head up high.

Obviously, there are some sports, such as golf or clay-pigeon shooting, where you are always solely in competition with yourself, unlike, say, tennis or rugby, where you directly interact with your opponents. Just imagine what would happen if you hit a golf ball and somebody hit it back; you'd never get it into the hole! Being in competition with yourself means setting your own goals and constantly moving towards them. What does it matter if you're last in the race if you have run your personal best time? You can be proud of what you've achieved and look forward to the next race, when perhaps someone else will finish behind you.

A good example is Dr Wayne Dyer, the author, who has run more than a dozen marathons and will cheerfully tell you that he's won them all.

'Come on, you didn't win,' a friend pointed out to him one day. 'How can you say that?'

Dr Dyer replied: 'It depends on how you define "win". Sure, there were others in the race who ran for two hours and ten minutes and then stopped, but anybody can do that. I kept on going for four and a half hours!'

5 I live in the present moment

'This is the only moment over which I have any control. I don't allow my mind to drift to regrets from the past and never put off until tomorrow that which I should be doing today. An opportunity missed today is gone forever.'

One of the main reasons why some people have difficulty concentrating is because they allow their minds to wander into the past or worry about what may happen in the future. Does worrying ever help you to get where you want to go? Of course it doesn't. Quite the opposite – it holds you back because you're not in the right mental state to deal with whatever's happening in the present effectively.

The most successful players are able to concentrate fully on what they're doing. They don't ponder upon past mistakes, even if they've only just occurred. Experienced players who make a bad shot will immediately run it through in their minds the way it should have been, then forget about it. They know that dwelling on errors will prevent them from playing the next shot as well as they could.

6 I am fearless, bold and courageous

'I have nothing to fear but fear itself. I will feel the fear and do it anyway.'

You've probably heard of the 'fight or flight' response to hazardous situations, which happens because our bodies are conditioned to respond to danger by pumping adrenalin into the bloodstream, arousing us to action. Obviously you need to feel energized when you're competing, as long as you're in control. But fear is a poor motivator. Far from exciting you to positive action, it freezes you. And, very often, the thing you're frightened of hasn't yet happened and, in all probability, never will.

7 I deserve to be successful

'Nobody is more deserving than I. I've worked for it. I want, believe and expect to win.'

Desire, belief and expectancy are not just good attitudes to have but are absolutely essential. Without them you won't stand a chance. Many sporting heroes never doubted that they would win; this belief in themselves (rather than in their physical attributes, talent or skill) gets results.

You, too, must believe that you deserve to win and not feel sorry for those you have defeated. They've done their best and you've done yours. What could be fairer than that?

8 Failure is not defeat

'Defeat is the decision to stop trying or to give up. There is no such thing as failure, only results. I learn from everything that happens to me, whether I succeed or not. In this way, I constantly improve.'

The way an athlete responds to losing is one of the marks of a true champion. How do you react when you're unsuccessful? Do you get discouraged, give up and feel sorry for yourself? Or do you pick yourself up, dust yourself down and start all over again, having learned from the experience? If you give up, you're doomed. Linford Christie was into his 30s before he tasted major success. If he had given up after every setback, he would never have become a great champion.

Never let discouragement throw you off course. You're bound to fall short of your target from time to time and, if you're wise, you'll analyse your disappointment, decide where you need to make corrections and get it right next time.

There are times when you have a bad game, but I look back on all the good times and tell myself that I am a good player and that it has to come right in the next match.

John Barnes, Liverpool footballer

9 I shall persist until I succeed

'I never give up. I know where I am going and, if I keep going long enough, I am certain to get there.'

Nigel Mansell missed out on winning the World Drivers' Championship several times, due to mechanical failures beyond his control, but kept going until he'd made it. Many do give up at the first sign of difficulty but these people are doomed to lives of mediocrity, envious of those who've done better but lacking the determination and perseverance to achieve for themselves.

There's nothing sadder than a person who's given up when they're almost in sight of their goal, who would have made it if only they'd kept going just a little longer. And the worst of it is that many will never know how close they were to realizing their dream.

10 I enjoy what I'm doing

'Life is a joy, filled with happiness. My enthusiasm knows no bounds. I am passionate about my sport, passionate about winning.'

We can't emphasize enough the need to enjoy what you're doing, including the process of preparing yourself and taking part. Enthusiasm spills over into every single thing you do. Without it, you're only half alive. Isn't it sad that many people don't have much enthusiasm for anything?

The sporting greats, almost without exception, truly love what they do. When they no longer get a kick out of it, either they start to lose and gradually fade from the top flight, or, if they've any sense, they retire. Many a star has packed it in simply because they weren't enjoying it any more. They realized they weren't going to be able to sustain the motivation to stay successful. As Martina Navratilova said: 'It's time for me to get on with the rest of my life.'

Ask yourself 'Do I really love what I'm doing?' Answer honestly. If it's 'no', try and find a way to inject some passion back into it. Begin by thinking about the parts you enjoy, then considering how you can expand them. Without passion, you won't enjoy what you're doing and you may as well admit that you're flogging a dead horse and do something else.

> *To be a member of a winning Ryder Cup team is some-thing any golfer should be prepared to walk across broken glass for.*
>
> Ian Woosnam, international golfer

When you're competing, training, or away from your sport altogether, repeat these ten headings to yourself frequently. They're called *affirmations*. This may sound fanciful at first but, if you repeat them often enough, they'll become deeply ingrained in your unconscious and you'll notice a growing sense of purpose and conviction. Your new attitudes will pave the way for the emotional changes which will enable you to manage your energy, respond to challenges more effectively and win more consistently!

9

Winning is All in the Mind

You can transform your life by changing your attitude.

Dynamic Living Principle No. 4

You may be wondering why we've included a chapter about the mind in a book on sport. After all, you don't need to know what's under the bonnet to drive a car, do you? As long as there's an engine that starts when you want it to, what more do you need? But, as any motor mechanic knows, it's not quite that simple. When you understand the basics, you drive with more skill and the engine will last longer. It's the same with the mind. You can make better use of it if you know a little about its workings. That's why we've packed this book full of ideas and techniques for unleashing the power of your mind to help you reach your goals.

Mind and body, body and mind – a very powerful combination. Many sports people know this intuitively but concentrate on developing their bodies without giving any attention to the other side of the equation. They spend hours exercising physically but rarely spend time training their minds!

One of the most remarkable demonstrations of mind power took place at a sports conference a few year ago. The psychologist and former weightlifter, Charles Garfield, asked some Soviet scientists to show him how performance could be improved using the mind. In the early hours of the morning, Garfield was taken to a gym. The Soviets asked him if he'd done any serious training recently. He hadn't. He'd kept in shape but hadn't practised in earnest for over a decade. They asked him to choose a lift and he decided on the bench press, which involves lying on your back and pushing a weight up to arms' length.

At first, straining for all he was worth, Garfield managed to bench press 136 kilograms (300 pounds), more than he'd lifted for many years. Then they asked him how much he would attempt if he was competing in an important competition that he was desperate to win. Garfield thought about it for a moment and then said that he would add 4.5 kilograms (10 pounds). The scientists took note.

He was then instructed to lie flat on his back, close his eyes and relax very deeply. He imagined his arms and legs becoming heavy and warm, then his chest and stomach releasing all the stress and tension, until he felt completely relaxed. After 40 minutes he was asked to sit up and look at the weights. While his eyes had been closed, the Soviets had added 30 kilograms (65 pounds) to the bar. 'There's no chance I can lift that,' he thought anxiously.

For the next 10 minutes, Garfield stared at the bar and mentally absorbed the image of the 166 kilograms (365 pounds). Then he lay on his back, eyes closed, while the scientists described vivid mental images of him lifting the weights. He imagined himself sitting in the stands, watching himself do the lift over and over again, until it was etched in his mind. Then, dozens of times, he saw himself making the lift, as if he were the person actually doing it. His instructors guided him as he imagined hearing the clink of the metal and the sound of his breathing, and feeling the pressure on his arms. After 20 minutes, they asked him to approach the bar and lift it for real.

He gave a mighty heave and made the lift just as easily as the 136 kilograms (300 pounds) earlier. Just 1 hour before, he'd told his instructors that he could probably manage an extra 4.5 kilograms (10 pounds). Now, to his amazement, he'd lifted 25 kilograms (55 pounds) more than that.

Garfield doesn't understand to this day how he did it but it taught him a very important lesson about mental rehearsal. If you imprint winning images into your mind at a deep enough level, you greatly increase your chances, providing, of course, that you have all the physical strength and skills you need.

Do you need further convincing? If so, we'd like to tell you about an experiment carried out in an American high school a few years ago. A number of students who were required to take physical education (PE) classes were divided into three groups. They were tested at basketball to see how many goals they could score from penalty throws. The first group scored 23 per cent, the second 21 per cent and the third 23 per cent. On average, they were scoring about one in five – not at all bad for occasional players.

For the next 4 weeks, the first group were told to go to the gym as normal during their PE lessons and practise penalty throws. This they did, every week, until they were re-tested at the end of the month. This time, they scored 45 per cent, an improvement of nearly 100 per cent.

Perhaps you're thinking that this was only to be expected; after all, take any ordinary group of people, get them to practise almost anything for a month and you'd see an improvement. But this is not the end of the story.

The second group were banned from the gym for a month. Instead, they had to spend the PE class away from the group, picturing themselves playing basketball. They were told to close their eyes and imagine all the sights, sounds and smells of the gym, and setting themselves up for a penalty throw. Then they had to see themselves shooting over and over again and, crucially, making every shot, i.e. scoring 100 per cent. They did this for 4 weeks and were then re-tested. This time they scored 40 per cent, nearly the same rate of improvement as the first group – even though they hadn't touched a basketball for a month!

What lesson can we learn from this? Clearly, that you can improve as much by practising in your mind as in the gym. But what happens if you do both? Well, the third group were asked to practise in the gym for 1 hour a day *and* visualize throwing at the basket for 1 hour every evening and scoring each time. When they were re-tested at the end of the month, they scored an incredible 66 per cent, nearly three times as many as they'd done at the start of the trial! We can assure you that many other experiments have given similar results.

Any professional athlete will tell you that mental training is equally as important as the physical. They mentally rehearse every move to complement their real-life practice. They don't have to be told that mental rehearsal adds power to their practice.

For example, once an Olympic pole vaulter was relaxing in his hammock on the morning of a big event when a reporter spotted him and went over to investigate. 'Raise the bar another notch,' said the pole vaulter, without opening his eyes. Somewhat taken aback, the reporter asked what he was doing. 'I'm practising,' came the reply!

We are going to tell you, in detail, how you can make your training more effective by making better use of your mind but first we're going to explain a little about how the mind functions. We'll start with a few simple concepts. The first is fundamental to everything.

Thoughts are things

We all have thoughts but have you ever stopped to wonder where they come from? The answer is simple: you put them there. Maybe you've never realized it but you choose which thoughts to allow into your mind, which to hold on to and which to release. And it's a fact that every action you take begins as a thought.

If you don't like a thought, you can change it. If it's a negative one, the sooner you change it, the better. Did you know that a single negative thought can bring about more than 100 biochemical changes in your body? Quite simply, if you don't control your thoughts, they're going to control you. Taking charge of your thoughts is the very first step to improving the mental side of your game.

The law of cause and effect

Every cause has an effect. Obviously, when a cricketer hits a four it's because his bat has connected with the ball hard enough to propel it to the boundary.

The blow (the cause) has made the ball move (the effect). Here's another example. When a boxer falls to the canvas, it's usually because his opponent has punched him hard enough in the right place to make him topple over. The punch is the cause, the effect is a horizontal boxer.

It may seem hard to believe at first but every 'cause' in your life began as a thought. Sometimes the thought is so fleeting, you're not even aware of it. Every time you blink, an unconscious thought has started a train of events which ends with the brain instructing the little muscles around your eyes to move. No thought – no action – wrong result; your eyes continue to feel uncomfortable.

Likewise, your emotions start out as thoughts. You cannot feel happy or sad, angry, guilty or hurt without first having a thought. Thoughts can make you healthy or ill, calm or agitated, confident or unsure. They can put you in the right frame of mind or ruin your concentration. It follows logically that, if you want the right results, you must think the right thoughts. It's a kind of chain reaction.

Once you have truly grasped the enormous power of thought you have taken a big step forward. Just reflect for a moment. Can you name even one event that ultimately did not have a thought as its cause? The truth is, you can't. It's impossible because there have never been any. And the good news is that you can use this insight to improve your performance. The secret is to allow only positive, confident thoughts to take root in your mind. Ask yourself: 'What must I think, believe and do every day, every minute, to become successful?' Then choose thoughts and beliefs that will help you in your quest.

Dr Wayne Dyer (see also page 65) provides a good example. He recalls his very first marathon. He'd heard about 'the Wall', when cramp hits you, but decided to train himself to focus his attention elsewhere and run right through it.

After 27 kilometres (17 miles), he was joined by another runner. 'You may be feeling alright now', said this negative thinker, 'but just you wait. You won't believe the pain that's going to hit you. I can tell by the way you're breathing that you've only got a couple of miles at the most.'

Dr Dyer politely told him he didn't want to listen to his kind of thinking and asked him to run with somebody else. Sure enough, 'Mr Negative' pulled a muscle after 35 kilometres (22 miles) and had to leave the race. Apparently, he'd entered over a dozen marathons and never completed one.

'How can I choose what to think?' you might ask. 'Isn't this a bit far fetched?' Try this exercise. Sit quietly for a few minutes and pay attention to the thoughts going through your mind. Just observe. Then listen out for negative thoughts, such as 'I can't', or 'I'm not good enough' and, whenever you become aware of one, tell it to go away. Shout 'Stop! Go away! Cancel!', or say it under your breath, and immediately replace it with the exact opposite, 'I can!' or 'Of course I'm good enough!' Become aware of your feelings now. Don't you feel more confident?

This technique is called *conscious thought stopping*. It brings you back to your senses whenever disempowering thoughts enter your mind. We'll return to it on page 83.

So now you know you *can* take control of your thoughts, let's look at the structure of the brain and piece together the next part of the jigsaw.

The left and right hemispheres of the brain

The brain has two hemispheres, each with its own individual functions. The *left brain* is the logical side. It controls use of language and numbers but it can only hold one thought at a time. If that thought happens to be negative, it has to be eliminated before a positive one can take its place.

The other hemisphere, the *right brain*, operates quite differently from the left. It is the creative, intuitive side. It senses rather than thinks and uses images rather than words or numbers. Unlike the left, it can deal with millions of pieces of information at a time. It is also the gateway to the unconscious mind – but more of this later (page 96).

How does this information relate to your sporting performance? Let's suppose you are a footballer. A team mate has just passed you the ball – what are you going to do with it? You scan the field. Your right brain senses the whereabouts of your team mates and the opposition, creating a picture of the situation in your mind. Almost instantaneously, it delves into your memory banks to see whether you've ever been in a similar situation before and whether you've learned anything that can help you this time. Meanwhile, your left brain is thinking, calculating, deciding. Then it will direct your legs and feet to pass the ball, shoot at goal, or whatever, while the right brain takes note and logs the results for future reference.

We know that most people have a tendency to favour one side or the other of the brain. We can usually spot 'left-brained' or 'right-brained' individuals. Most accountants, librarians and lawyers rely heavily on the left side of their brains. Successful artists, musicians and inventors make full use of the right side of their brains.

So what of the mind? This is not the same as the brain and it's important not to confuse the two. The brain is nothing more than a small computer-like mechanism weighing about 1.4 kilograms (3 pounds). The mind, though, can't be seen, touched or smelt. It can't be measured, or operated upon by a surgeon's knife. It is the soul, the inner person, the seat of intelligence and thought.

Like the brain, the mind is more than a single entity. It's rather like an iceberg floating in the sea, with 10 per cent visible above the surface and the other 90 per cent hidden below the water. The seen and unseen parts represent . . .

The conscious and unconscious minds

Psychologists, like sports fans, argue about most things but there's one point the majority agree on – that most of our mental processing takes place below the level of consciousness. This is actually a very good thing. Imagine if you had consciously to instruct your heart to beat or your stomach to digest your food. Luckily, your unconscious mind takes care of all that so you can direct your attention to other, more fulfilling concerns, but it also does much, much more.

For instance, the outstanding basketball player, Larry Bird, was hired to appear in a soft-drinks commercial in which he was required to miss the basket. The habit of scoring was so deeply programmed into his unconscious mind that he scored nine jump shots in a row before he could bring himself to miss!

Although you are not aware of it minute by minute, the unconscious is actually the most powerful part of your mind. Like the bulk of the iceberg, you can't see it but you know it's there. It works unceasingly, even when you're asleep. But it has one major drawback: it is conditioned by all the experiences you've had, ever since the day you were born. Your memories, fears, attitudes and habits are all programmed in, influencing your behaviour quietly and with devastating effects.

What would you say if we told you there was a simple yet effective way of accessing your unconscious and changing your conditioning? As we've said, the Soviet bloc coaches knew how. Wouldn't you want to learn their secrets, so that you can create the right unconscious thought processes and, quite literally, transform your performance on the sportsfield? Of course you would.

Well, we've got news for you. There is a fairly simple way. It involves going into a pleasant, relaxed state known as . . .

Alpha level

The conscious mind will continually chatter away, racing from one thought to the next, unless it is quietened down so that your unconscious can come to the fore. Fortunately, this can be accomplished fairly easily by getting into a dreamy, relaxed state known as *alpha level*, the state between being fully awake and fully asleep through which we all pass twice a day, morning and night. Once you've reached alpha level, you can access your unconscious mind.

In alpha, the brain's rate of vibration drops, the two hemispheres are in harmony and you can perform any mental activity more efficiently. The *critical censor*, which normally stops your unconscious mind accepting new ideas, shuts down. Now, you can re-programme your unconscious without interference.

Let's take a moment to show you exactly what we mean. It's the night before a big match. Tomorrow, you're playing tennis against the current champion, who you've never beaten. You're in bed, dozing off. Your left brain is racing and chasing as usual: 'I haven't a hope. I can't. This person always beats me. I'll never do it.' These thoughts go straight into your unconscious where they are stored in your memory. From here they will influence your performance the next day.

Now, imagine yourself feeling very, very relaxed. Your body is completely at ease, with no strain or tension at all. You feel a little light-headed, almost as if your body is no longer a part of you, a sure sign you've reached alpha level. Slowly tell yourself, over and over again: 'I can do it. The past is the past. I know I can win this time. I feel confident.' Add, for good measure: 'My opponent is not a good as he [or she] used to be and has many weaknesses [make a list of them]. I am playing better than ever before.'

If it were daytime and you were fully awake, your conscious mind would retort: 'Don't be so silly. Of course you won't win. What makes you think this time will be any different?' But in alpha, the positive messages you have chosen to feed into the unconscious will get through. It will accept your suggestions as reality. 'But,' you might say, 'surely my mind knows that I'm making it all up. It won't be fooled by a few white lies.' Your conscious mind knows but your unconscious does not. It cannot distinguish between thoughts and so-called 'real' events. Try the following exercise.

Close your eyes and imagine you are hungry and have a plate of your favourite food in front of you. Sense the smell, the sight. Now take a bite. Enjoy the taste. Is your mouth watering? Of course! But why? You know it's only your imagination, don't you? And yet your taste buds are responding as if the food is very real.

The truth is that your unconscious mind cannot tell the difference between information coming from your five senses, and your thoughts and mental images. If you imagine that you are running a marathon vividly enough, your unconscious will accept it as a fact. How many times have you woken from a bad dream, panicking, convinced that a nightmare is reality? It's the same principle. Remember Dynamic Living Principle No. 2: 'You create your own reality with your thoughts, feelings and attitudes'.

Another way of looking at this principle is summed up in a useful and memorable phrase . . .

The thinker thinks and the prover proves

The mind has a way of convincing itself that it is right. If an idea seems reasonable, and the mind accepts it as true, it tends to become reality. In other words, if you think you can't do something and you *expect* to fail, you inevitably will. But if you think you can, and expect to succeed, you are likely to do just that.

When you are wondering whether you are capable or not, it's almost as if there are two voices in your head chattering away to each other. If the *thinker*, which operates from the conscious mind, thinks: 'I'm no good at this, I can't do it', the *prover*, housed in the unconscious, sets to work making it come true. Then, when it doesn't work out, you find yourself thinking: 'You see, I was right, I couldn't do it.'

Sports fans have seen this happening time and time again. Take, for instance, an international cricket team whose players lose their confidence one summer – it could be in the final of the World Cup – then lose a few matches, are severely criticized in the Press, lose their self-belief and consequently play even worse. They become the butt of cruel jokes and are branded a national disgrace. Once this happens, it's extremely difficult to get back to winning ways. It's usually necessary to drop many of the old players and bring in new blood.

If you allow the thinker to dwell on the idea that you are a useless player, the prover will make sure you won't be surprised by the result. If you genuinely want to be a winner at sport, or anything else, you must be in control of the thinker. Remember, right thoughts lead to right action, so *take charge of your thoughts.*

A word of encouragement

You need a deep-seated belief that you *can* win and you're *going* to win, and it's not enough to try and convince yourself in your rational, conscious mind – it must penetrate your unconscious. Once an idea takes root there, the unconscious will do everything it can to bring it into reality. This is one of the 'laws' of applied psychology, observed and proven to be true throughout recorded history. Two of the most important such laws are set out below. Once you're familiar with them, you can use them to your advantage.

The law of belief

Whatever you believe, with emotion, becomes your reality. At this moment, you are the result of all the beliefs you have ever held. The beliefs you hold now will determine what you become in the future.

The law of expectancy

Whatever you expect, with confidence, becomes your own self-fulfilling prophecy. You continually act as your own fortune-teller by the way you talk to yourself. What you think will happen inevitably will.

Now that you understand how your mind works, you have all the background information you need to take charge of your destiny by taking control of your thoughts. It's not that difficult but it does take practice and persistence. You will have to be constantly on your guard against negative thinking and self-doubt but, after a while, it becomes easier and easier until you are automatically and unconsciously being positive. Then the exciting part begins – you notice your performance, and your results, improving! The next three chapters give you all the techniques you need.

10

Developing Winning Mental Skills

The mind is the limit. As long as the mind can envision the fact that you can *do something, you can do it as long as you really do believe it 100 per cent.*

Arnold Schwarzenegger, body-builder and film star

You'd be amazed if you knew just how little attention some sports people give to exercising the most important muscle in their bodies – the one between their ears. Anyone who makes this mistake is doomed to mediocrity; similarly, teams who ignore mental training are easily spotted – in the lower reaches of the league table, unable to achieve the consistency needed to win promotion.

Mental toughness is usually the deciding factor. Top athletes know how to take charge of their thoughts and control their emotions, and every single one of us can learn how to do the same. Like all skills, it takes practice but it's well worth the effort.

A competent coach will teach all the physical techniques until they become habitual and automatic but a top-class coach knows that some of the most important practice is done in the mind. Make sure you don't fall into the trap of devoting all your energy to purely physical matters. Complement all your other efforts with mental training, which will strengthen your positive thinking and positive emotions for positive results.

Your mental training programme

We're going to describe some effective techniques that will fine-tune your mental skills. The results will literally astound you.

Your six-step programme

1 Relax your body deeply.
2 Develop awareness and mindfulness.

3 Examine your beliefs.

4 Take charge of your thinking.

5 Get a grip on your emotions.

6 Use positive mental imagery.

We'll cover Steps 5 and 6 in Chapters 11 and 12, so let's get started with relaxation, beliefs and taking charge of your thinking. Remember, the key to success is practising these skills until they are deeply ingrained in your unconscious mind. You can speed up the process by quietening the conscious mind. It's quite simple to do. The secret is to . . .

1 Relax your body deeply

To access your unconscious, you must relax the physical body completely. What do you understand by 'relaxation' in this instance? Does the word conjure up images of lounging in a comfortable chair, having a drink, watching television or nattering to friends? All these activities are relaxing but not to the extent we're thinking of. When we talk of relaxation, it's a very much deeper level of letting go and unwinding.

When you deliberately relax, your muscles go limp and floppy as tension is released, your breathing becomes calm and regular and your heartbeat and circulation slow. Your mind becomes tranquil and serene. You feel almost as if your body is no longer a part of you. Then a strange thing happens. You begin to be more aware of yourself and your surroundings. Perhaps you didn't notice the ticking of the clock before but now you do. The traffic in the street may be louder than before; but it won't disturb you because you can't be bothered to let it. Then you can actually listen to your thoughts almost as if you are eavesdropping on your own internal dialogue.

You must be totally comfortable before you start. Make sure your head and neck are supported. Avoid all interruptions and sit quietly by yourself in a warm and peaceful place. Close your eyes, notice your breathing and focus your attention on each part of the body, in sequence, until you feel it go limp and heavy, perhaps even a little warm. When your body begins to feel a little detached and your mind starts to drift, you are there. We teach two main ways of achieving this, *tensing and relaxing* and *autogenics*, although there are many more. We suggest that you choose the one which works best for you.

Tensing and relaxing

Each time you breathe in, tense a group of muscles as hard as you can for a count of five. Start with your feet, your calves, knees, thighs and buttocks. Slowly move up to your stomach, chest and shoulders. Then relax your arms and hands, and neck and face muscles. Each time you breathe out, silently whisper the word 'relax' or 'calm'. Feel the tension melting away, the tightness flowing out of each part of your body, leaving your muscles floppy and loose. Now notice the difference between tension and relaxation. Enjoy the feeling of warmth and heaviness as it spreads from the tips of your toes all the way up to the top of your head.

Now count slowly down from ten to one, saying the words 'deeper and deeper' as you do so. When you get to one, imagine yourself in a very relaxing place, somewhere safe and peaceful where you find it easy to drift off into a very restful state. Perhaps you feel most at peace lying on a beach, aware of the sound of the waves lapping gently on the sand, with the warm sun caressing your body. Or in a beautiful garden, surrounded by flowers and shrubs, with a sparkling stream flowing gently into a rock pool. Or in the sitting room of a quaint country cottage, with heavy curtains shutting out the cold and a flickering coal fire, listening to the sound of the rain beating on the window panes.

Forget reality and let the world take care of itself for 20 minutes or so while you enjoy this peaceful feeling and do your mental exercises.

Autogenic relaxation

Autogenic relaxation was invented by Dr Johannes Schultz and adopted with outstanding results by Dr Georgi Lozanov in his pioneering work with the Soviet bloc athletes; this was the method taught to Charles Garfield, as we described on page 69. The full procedure is rather lengthy but you can learn a shortened version which gives excellent results for most people.

Make yourself comfortable, close your eyes, then silently say the phrases to yourself, slowly, in sequence:

My right hand is heavy and relaxed.

My left hand is heavy and relaxed.

My right arm is heavy and relaxed.

My left arm is heavy and relaxed.

My arms are heavy and warm.

Warmth is flowing into my hands.

Do this also for your feet and legs, then your stomach and chest, shoulders and neck.

Say each phrase two or three times. As you do so, gently focus your mind on the area of the body to which you are referring. Allow each part (except the forehead) to feel heavy, warm and relaxed. Notice the warmth and heaviness spreading as the desired effect takes hold.

Finally, repeat the following phrases two or three times:

My heart beat is strong and regular.

My breathing is calm and regular; I am at peace.

My body breathes me.

My forehead is cool and clear.

I am at peace.

Now, with each breath, slowly count backwards from ten to one, saying the words 'deeper and deeper' between each number. When you get to one, imagine yourself in a very relaxing place, in exactly the same way as you would if you were using the tensing and relaxing method.

It's best to do your relaxation in silence but you might find it helpful to listen to some relaxing music, such as the slow movements from the Baroque classics (Bach, Vivaldi, Corelli, Handel, etc.) or a piece of modern relaxation music. If you find relaxation difficult at first, don't worry; most of the problems will disappear with regular practice. In time, you will be able to relax in just a few seconds, such as during a critical moment during a tense match.

2 Develop awareness and mindfulness

When you're completely and utterly relaxed, it's almost as if you're entirely detached from your own thoughts and feelings, so use this valuable time to observe what's going on in your mind. Listen to the incessant chattering of your thoughts, which we call the *internal dialogue*. Be aware of any negative-thinking patterns, such as self-doubt or unhelpful criticism. If you experience any negative emotions make a note of them. You will learn how to deal with them later.

Remember, your performance is directly affected by your attitudes and beliefs which, in turn, are directly affected by your thinking. Passively observe your thoughts and you will instinctively know where you are going wrong. Change your thinking, and your attitudes and beliefs will also change. Right cause – right effect. Right thinking – right results.

3 Examine your beliefs

It's not the situations and events that shape our lives but our beliefs about them. Winners don't believe in luck. They believe that they are responsible for creating their own results and that nothing is down to fate or fortune. You may feel we've laboured the point in previous chapters but it's with good reason; it is absolutely vital to get your beliefs on your side. If you keep telling yourself that you can be successful and refuse to listen to anyone who tries to convince you that you'll fail, you'll improve your chances immeasurably.

Any belief which affects your self-confidence influences your ability to win. It doesn't even matter if the belief is true or not. Why not? Well, first of all, it's usually hard to prove a belief one way or the other in any case. But what is even more crucial is whether your beliefs help or hinder you. As we have seen, beliefs can empower or disable you. Positive beliefs enable you to make full use of your talents, negative beliefs programme your brain to fail. If you don't believe you can win, you can't.

We'd like you to take a few minutes right now to list your beliefs about your sporting ability. Group them into two categories: empowering and disempowering beliefs. The first group often begins with words such as 'I can', and 'I will'. The second includes 'I can't', 'I'm unlucky at' and 'I'm not as good as'.

Now take each of your disempowering beliefs and consider how it first came about and why you still hang on to it. Was it something your parents or teachers used to say to you when you were a child? Or something you once read, or saw on television? Dispute it: is there any evidence that it might contain a ring of truth?

Negative beliefs can nearly always be traced back to a time when you were small and someone made an unfortunate remark which you took to heart. So the next step is to take each of your disempowering beliefs in turn, change it into a positive and write it down. For example, change 'I can't' to 'I can' and 'I'm not very good at' to 'If I apply myself to . . . , I can be as good as anyone else'.

Now write down as many reasons as you can why your new belief is true. Where's the evidence? Perhaps you've already enjoyed a great deal of success or are accurately modelling yourself on someone who has. What are your particular strengths? What experiences have you had that back up your new belief? Have you read any inspiring books about people like yourself who have become successful? If they can do it, why not you? Every reason you can come up with adds power to your new belief system and, every time you write it down, it is imprinted more deeply into your mind. You're on your way to wiping out those old tapes and replacing them with the new recordings you need and want. Remember, every single thought sparks off a chain of events that leads inevitably to some result, whether that be a triumph or a catastrophe. So let's speed up the process and . . .

Take charge of your thinking

You cannot prevent thoughts from entering your head but you certainly can notice them, sift them and drive out the ones you don't want. If you are quick off the mark, the damaging thought will drift harmlessly away. But if you allow it to linger for, say, 30 seconds or more, it will permeate your unconscious. How can you get rid of negative thoughts and replace them with positives? There are three very effective ways which we urge you to practise until they have become habits: conscious thought stopping, the seven-day mental diet and affirmations.

Conscious thought stopping

We told you about conscious thought stopping in the last chapter (p. 73). You'll remember it as the act of stopping a negative thought from taking root in your mind and it's one of the most useful techniques you can learn. Start by taking a short break several times a day, sitting quietly and paying attention to your thoughts. You can easily do it at home, in the office, or wherever you happen to be. Every time a thought pops into your head, ask yourself: 'Is it positive or negative? Constructive or destructive?' If it's negative, shoo it away and replace it with its opposite. Keep doing this until it becomes a habit. In time, warning bells will sound or a red light will flash in your mind as your 'negative-thought alert' springs into action.

Seven-day mental diet

When you've grasped the idea, you can go on a *Seven-day mental diet*. This is just as effective at clearing out your mental system as a raw juice diet is at cleaning out your internal organs. Begin when you're reasonably certain the time is right and you're committed to seeing it through. Then follow the three simple rules set out below.

Rule 1 For the next 7 consecutive days, reject all negative, disempowering thoughts or feelings, veto any unresourceful words or phrases and refuse to focus your attention on failure, problems or defeat. Tell yourself that you are not allowed to worry about anything for more than 30 seconds at a time, at most.

Rule 2 If you should find yourself taken unawares by a negative thought or feeling, instantly use thought stopping to cancel it, then immediately replace it with a positive one.

Rule 3 If you backslide, don't chastise yourself. It won't be a problem for you if you deal with it immediately but, if you continue to focus on it for 30 seconds or more, you must wait until the following morning and start again. No matter how far through the week you are, you must go back to Day One and start counting all over again.

You'll find that you've ingrained a healthy new habit into your consciousness once you've completed the Seven-day mental diet. You'll find it easy to constantly check on your level of positivity. Then you can move on to the next step, which is learning to use affirmations.

Affirmations

An *affirmation* is a solemn declaration of intent which focusses your attention on how you want things to be. This is crucial because, once the brain is locked on to what you don't want, it's almost impossible to break away. Your task is constantly to give yourself empowering suggestions so that your mind comes to your assistance.

Affirmations are widely used by professional sportsmen and sportswomen, and they really work. A few years ago, a leading tennis player, Tom Gullickson, had a serious problem with his game: he went to pieces during tie-breakers and was losing matches he should have won against weaker opponents. Gullickson consulted a sports psychologist who told him to repeat every day, 30 times or more, 'I love tie-breakers', and to paste little stickers all over his house with the same message. He was rather dubious but did as suggested.

Two weeks later, he called the psychologist to say he'd at last won a tie-breaker but he added that it was nothing to do with the affirmations or those 'silly bits of paper'. A few weeks later, he rang to say he'd won two tie-breakers and gone on to win a tight match (although it was obviously unrelated to all that nonsense). Before long, he found himself thinking 'If I can only get to a tie-breaker, I'll win this set' during matches. After that, Gullickson's performance in tie-breakers was outstanding. Looking back, he admits to being aware that something about his attitude and confidence had changed. It was a turning point in his career.

You, too, can easily get good results by using affirmations and you can add to their power in several ways. Try taking several deep breaths and relaxing into alpha level before reciting your positive statements at least ten times. Repeat them when your unconscious is most receptive, such as first thing in the morning and just before you go to sleep at night.

Reciting affirmations when in alpha is called *autosuggestion* and is one of the most rapid methods of re-programming your unconscious and bringing the affirmation into reality.

Then close your eyes and get a clear mental picture that makes you feel successful and imagine yourself experiencing strong, joyful emotions. It's really very simple as long as you follow five basic rules. We call these rules *the five Ps*.

The five Ps

1 Present tense Always state your affirmations in the present tense. Use sentence stems such as 'I am', 'I can', and 'I achieve', not 'I will', or 'I intend to'. If you were to tell your unconscious that you 'will be successful', it will assume that you can postpone your success to a future date. Tell it 'I am successful' and it will make it a priority.

2 Personal Start your affirmations with the word 'I', not 'You' or 'He' or 'We'. Your unconscious is only responsible for you – it cannot work on behalf of anyone else.

3 Positive Your unconscious sometimes overlooks a negative word in a sentence. If you were to say 'I will not lose', it might ignore the 'not', and what would be left? Instead, say 'I will win'. The rule is 'Never say never' and 'Don't say don't'.

4 Powerful Summon all the emotional power you can muster by using a persuasive tone of voice and speaking your affirmations with conviction. Other people wouldn't take notice of a weak and weedy voice, so why should the inner you? Say 'I *can* do it', 'I *am* a winner', etc. as if you really mean it.

5 Practise Practice makes permanent. Persist and you will succeed.

Suggestions have power! An African witchdoctor can cause a person to die instantly by 'pointing the bone' and casting a spell. The very suggestion is enough to kill him because he believes without question that the witchdoctor has this power. Western doctors use suggestions too. If you've ever heard of placebos (pills and potions which contain no active ingredients), you'll know that doctors often prescribe them knowing that patients will benefit simply because they believe they will.

You can add further power to your affirmations in a number of ways. Write them on a card and carry them around with you. Read them through frequently. Write them on sticky labels and paste them to your bathroom mirror and fridge door. Record them on to a cassette tape and listen to it every day when you are in a receptive frame of mind. Above all practise! Using affirmations is a little like dripping white paint into a tin of black paint – it only makes a small difference at first but, if you keep at it, the paint will gradually become grey, then white. Similarly, drop positive thoughts into your mental bucket and your attitude will gradually become more positive.

Examples of affirmations which can be used for various purposes are:

● To build into yourself the qualities you need:

I shall persist until I succeed.

I am dedicated, determined, patient and enthusiastic.

I have confidence in my abilities.

I am strong and healthy and full of energy.

● To foster positive mental attitudes:

I think, talk and act positively at all times.

I am deserving of success.

I'm getting more and more enthusiastic about accomplishing my goals.

I overcome all obstacles.

I am a strong and worthy person.

● To speed up your progress:

Every day, in every way, I'm getting better and better.

I am getting closer and closer every day to achieving my goals.

● To correct problems during the contest:

I love tie-breakers.

I always score from the penalty spot.

I know I can do it.

I am full of energy. I feel fresh and strong.

Getting a Grip on Your Emotions

We promise according to our hopes and perform according to our fears.

La Rochefoucauld, French writer (1613–80)

There is a direct connection between your energy level and performance and your emotions; when you're in tune with your emotions, your game seems effortless. Top athletes learn how to trigger positive emotions because they know they will not be at their best unless they're in the right emotional state. You feel different according to whether you're happy, angry, sad or fearful, which isn't surprising because you *are* different. Your body chemistry and every cell in your body change along with your emotions and feelings. Isn't that astonishing?

Next time you are watching sport, see if you can spot how the players react to pressure. You'll see some (usually inexperienced) players performing as if they've withdrawn emotionally from the contest. If things aren't going their way, they just go through the motions. They stop taking chances, and risk losing, not because they lack talent or skill but simply because they've stopped caring. Unless they can get a grip on themselves, they might as well pack up and go home, because they have, in effect, already conceded defeat. This reaction to pressure is called *tanking*.

Others get angry. Anger is high, negative energy. Some people mistakenly think that it gets you fired-up and makes you try harder. Perhaps; but angry people are usually so focussed on their anger that they are blind to what's going on around them. They're no longer in control of themselves; their concentration goes and they squander their energy on unproductive activities – energy which would be better channelled into beating their opponent. In a nutshell, you can get angry *or* rise to the challenge in a measured, controlled way but you can't do both. What you want is controlled aggression, not intense, uncoordinated anger. The cost to your system is too great.

My coach has helped me to understand my nature – calm,
not prone to tempers, taking everything in my stride.
Many top athletes crack under pressure, but for me
the more the better.

Sally Gunnell, Olympic 400-metres hurdles gold medallist

Unless, of course, you're John McEnroe. He was probably the only recent champion who was able to cope with pressure by getting angry *and* maintaining his concentration at the same time. His behaviour had spin-offs of course, especially in unsettling less experienced opponents. Pat Cash, who played him many times, claimed that McEnroe was never angry for more than a split second. If he saw his opponent was rattled, he would feign anger for the rest of the match until he won. In other words, he knew how to use his emotions perfectly as a tactical device. It didn't work on everybody of course – the more experienced were obviously too skilled at managing their own emotions to allow his antics to bother them. But McEnroe was unusual. You'd be a very rare person if you could do the same.

Another common response to pressure is to become so overpowered by nerves that you can't manage the stress, no matter how badly you want to. You battle on bravely, even though you feel quite overwhelmed by the situation. This is *choking*. The desire to win is still there but you need some time to get yourself back together again. If you don't take charge of your emotions quickly enough, there's a danger of becoming angry or tanking, both of which would make you even less effective.

It's very important to realize that nerves aren't actually a bad thing; what matters is how you handle them. One player might have an uncomfortable feeling in her stomach and call it 'fear'; another might call it 'excitement'. Even the top sports stars feel a touch of anxiety before a big event but they've learned to utilize it better than the rest.

You need the energy to meet the challenges you face, which means engaging positive emotions so you can cope with the pressure *and* enjoy it. In other words, you need to stay on the left side of the energy/emotions table (see page 39) and be able to move rapidly from the low-energy state to high and back again at will. How are you going to achieve this?

Well, first of all, realize that your emotions are there to serve you, not to ruin your chances. Think of them as a warning signal. They are nature's way of telling you that something is wrong and that you need to take some sort of action. What's the message they are sending you? Listen to it and act upon it.

You are either looking at things incorrectly or doing something wrongly. So if, for example, you are feeling angry or worried or discouraged, be aware that you are out of kilter and need to regain your emotional balance.

Ways to change your mood – instantly

Top stars are continually aware of their feelings at any particular moment. They know how to change their emotional state instantly and you must learn to do the same. No ifs or buts. It's vital to get a grip on your emotions. We're going to give you four effective methods to help you do this whenever you need to. You'll learn how to tackle negative feelings from both the mental and physical angles, and literally to talk yourself out of a bad mood.

Four ways to change your mood instantly

1 Use your physiology.

2 Re-focus your attention.

3 Positive self-talk.

4 Positive questions.

I Use your physiology

Try this experiment. Let your shoulders slump, scowl at the floor and allow the corners of your mouth to droop so that you're a picture of misery. How do you feel? Tired? Anxious? Depressed? Awful? Now stand tall, chin up, head erect, looking straight in front of you, shoulders back, and put a big smile on your face. Now isn't that better? Suddenly you feel alert, powerful and happy. (If you don't, you're a rare exception.) It's an intriguing fact that if you act as if you are happy, then you will become happy. But, conversely, if you act as if you are tired, you will become tired. So, if you are feeling, say, afraid, act as if you are courageous and adopt a courageous stance; you will be surprised how quickly your mood changes. To quote the title of a best-selling book by Susan Jeffers, *Feel the Fear and Do it Anyway.*

Changing your physiology is the first of our mood-controlling techniques. It consists of adopting the posture you would have if you were feeling the way you want to. Let's say you are feeling a little down in the dumps when you need to be alert and ready for action. How would you be standing if you were already feeling alert? How would you hold your head and shoulders? What would your facial expression be? Try changing your posture.

If you want to feel aggressive, adopt an aggressive stance. If you're not sure what an aggressive stance is, invent one. Clench your fists, tense your muscles, thrust out your jaw. Bring the full force of your breathing and tone of voice to bear at the same time; grunt, growl, curse or whatever feels right for you.

You can use your physiology to change how you are feeling any time you like. Let's say you are feeling tired towards the end of a match. You are in the lead but beginning to doubt that you have enough energy to hang on for victory. Consciously act as if the game has just begun and you are feeling as fresh as a racehorse champing at the bit just before the 3.45. At the same time, dismiss all thought of tiredness from your mind by thought stopping, run through some affirmations and use the other techniques described below – re-focussing, positive self-talk and positive questions. You'll find your tiredness evaporating and affecting you no longer.

Another way of changing your mood is to have a good laugh. Nothing relieves stress more quickly. When you laugh, your facial muscles tighten and relax, your breathing deepens and you suddenly feel more energized. Many sports stars have a tremendous sense of humour and instinctively use it to take the heat out of difficult situations before bringing their attention back to the serious business of winning.

For example, in 1987, the Denver Broncos were playing the Cleveland Browns for a place in the Superbowl. Cleveland were one touchdown ahead. With less than 2 minutes to go, the Broncos were pushed back to their 1½-yard line. Everyone, including the Broncos players, huddled in their own end zone, assumed they had lost. In this impossible situation, one of them, Keith Bishop, looked at his team mates and said: 'Hey, now we've got them just where we want them!' The mood changed in an instant. Despondency lifted. One of the players laughed so hard he fell over. The gloom and doom was instantly replaced by calm and confidence. Amazingly, as soon as play re-started, the Broncos drove the length of the field and scored with seconds to go. They eventually went on to win in extra time.

If you are one of those people who has trouble seeing the funny side of things, you are probably overstressed and need to work hard on the techniques in this chapter. There's a funny side to anything, if you're willing to look for it!

2 Re-focus your attention

Often, the best thing you can do when you're in a tight situation is direct your thoughts to what's *right* about it, rather than dwelling on what's not so good. Here's an example. You've played 10 minutes of an important football match and the other team scores. How do you feel? Sorry for yourself? 'Oh no, that's it! Ten minutes gone and they're ahead already! We haven't a chance now.'

Do you think the most successful teams think this way? Of course they don't. They focus on something positive about the situation and mentally accentuate it. If someone makes a mistake, they re-frame it (see page 102). Compare this internal dialogue with the above: 'We're going to keep battling and maintain our composure. There's ten minutes gone, and that leaves eighty more to regain control, assert our superiority and win the match. We can do it.' Re-focussing your attention in this way sends powerful signals to your brain that you're not going to lie down and play dead.

Similarly, top golfers always concentrate on the hole they are playing and dismiss any previous mistakes from their minds completely. You must do the same. If you had problems with a particular hole last time you played the course, forget it! You're literally heading for defeat if you approach a shot thinking: 'There's that bunker. Last week, I hit the ball straight into it. Better play it safe this time'. What do you think would be likely to happen? One of two things. Either you'll land up in the bunker again or you'll over-compensate and hit the ball into the rough on the other side of the fairway.

So what's the solution? It's simple. Focus entirely on the hole. Remember, if you can see obstacles, it's because you've taken your eye off the goal.

Norman Vincent Peale, author of *The Power of Positive Thinking*, was out playing golf one day when he hit the ball into the rough.

'It's going to be tough getting out of here', he said to his partner.

His friend smiled. 'Didn't I read something about positive thinking in one of your books?' he said.

Shame-faced, Dr Peale had to admit that he had.

'Then you mustn't be so negative. Do you think you could play a good shot if the ball was in the short grass on the fairway?'

Dr Peale thought that he could.

'Well, the rough is only mental. It's only rough because you think it is. If you think the obstacle is too big to overcome, it will defeat you, but with the right attitude and a good swing of the club, you'll play exactly the shot you want.'

Dr Peale focussed his attention on the ball, repeated the phrase 'The rough is only mental', and hit the ball smoothly on to the green.

At its simplest, concentration is nothing more than focussed attention. Your conscious mind cannot deal with more than one thing at a time, so, when you focus, you cut out all the extraneous sounds and confusion going on around you. Watch a rugby player taking a penalty – head down, staring at the ball, then the posts, then the ball again, visualizing it heading straight between the posts and over the bar. It's a little like putting blinkers on a racehorse so it can only focus on the course ahead of it and is therefore less distracted by the crowd and the other horses.

One way of making sure you concentrate on what you're doing is to 'speak it out'. For example, if a rugby player practising spot kicks were to say 'kick' at the exact moment his foot strikes the ball, his attention would be riveted on just that. A golfer practising his strokes could say 'back' and 'hit' as he lifts and swings the club and makes contact with the ball. The very act of speaking out what you're doing gives a powerful focus for mind and body which can counterbalance feelings of doubt and uncertainty. If you're a footballer, try saying 'score' to yourself next time you shoot at goal.

You can use re-focussing at any time, whether you're training, competing or relaxing. Once you've got into the habit of listening to your inner dialogue and being aware of your feelings, you know when you need to make changes. Always look for something positive to focus on, give it all your attention and keep your mind on what you want. It's one of the most effective ways of taking charge of your emotions.

3 Positive self-talk

Another way of regaining control of your mood is by paying attention to the language you use. Words have power. *Positive self-talk* means replacing mildly positive words with stronger ones and potentially harmful negative words with any that soften their impact.

Here are some examples. Suppose you are about to take part in an important competition, one that you have really set your heart on winning. Imagine how you would feel. Merely all right? Happy? Confident? Motivated? Strong? Determined? Say each of these words aloud, slowly, in sequence. What's happening in your body? How do you feel mentally? Are you raring to go? Perhaps you are, perhaps you aren't.

Now, repeat the following words, slowly, one at a time, and see how you feel: 'Terrific.' 'Ecstatic.' 'Unstoppable.' 'Driven.' 'Invincible.' 'Resolved.' Feel how the emotion is intensified. You're not just confident now but irresistible!

These are examples of how you can intensify a good feeling. However, you can also use positive self-talk to take the sting out of a negative sensation. Next time you are feeling 'angry', 'exhausted' or 'stressed', try softening the language you use. Tell yourself you are 'a little miffed', 'a bit weary' or 'somewhat tense'. Observe your reaction. You'll find the emotion becoming less extreme and, as a result, you'll feel less disabled by it.

Any sports person who says they don't feel nervous before a big match is probably being economical with the truth. They feel stress just like the rest of us but know how to handle it and channel it into an improved performance. Top performers know how to talk to themselves so that they stay in control of their emotions continually, and some even make up a tune to go with the words and hum it to themselves. Correctly handled, stress is the force that propels you to success. Imagine Olympic sprinters, in training, going for a gentle jog around the track, taking their time! They'd never be able to compete at the highest level.

No, it's not the stress that causes you problems but the way you deal with it. If you feel tension in your stomach and start to sweat before the contest and use words like 'nervous' or 'anxious' to describe it, you are causing yourself problems. Why not call it 'high energy' or 'excitement' instead? Take your cue from the theatrical world, where they say: 'It's okay to have butterflies in your stomach as long as they fly in formation!'

Everyone has their own favourite words which enhance positive emotions. Vocabulary varies from person to person, region to region and even sport to sport. It pays to develop your own list of words for use whenever you feel the need for a change of mood.

4 Positive questions

One of the quickest ways to change how you feel is to ask yourself different questions. 'What do you mean, ask yourself different questions? I wasn't asking myself any questions in the first place!' you might say. Ha! You've just asked yourself a question without even realizing it and you're doing it all the time. The problem with questions is this: whatever question you ask, your brain will give you an answer, even if the question itself has no basis in reality. So if you ask a negative question, the answer you get will reinforce what you *don't* want.

Here's an example. You've just lost – again – to an opponent who always seems to beat you. 'Why can't I win against X?' you ask yourself. 'Why is he so much better than me?'

'Because you're no good,' comes the reply. 'You're not as talented, and he's stronger than you.' Now you're feeling really down in the dumps. You've convinced yourself that you'll never stand a chance and wonder if it will even be worth turning up next time.

If you know anything about computers, you'll have heard of the *GIGO* concept, *Garbage In, Garbage Out*. It's just the same with the questions you ask of yourself. If the question is flawed, so will be the answer. How can you turn this around? Well, think about this question: 'How can I make sure I beat him next time?' This time, your brain has a more constructive question to pon- der and it will throw up constructive answers. 'Use different tactics.' 'Practise your second serve/tee shot/finishing/starting/defensive play.' 'Rehearse this shot so I won't be caught unawares again.' You're not only in a better frame of mind but you've got something definite to work on.

Of course, answers won't always pop into your head instantly and they might come when least expected. This is your unconscious mind at work. You may be doing something else entirely when a promising idea comes to you, or you may be watching television or reading a book when you spot something that might help. The trick is to be alert and notice when this happens.

You can start asking yourself deliberately positive questions from the moment you get up in the morning. 'What can I do to improve today?' 'How can I inject some fun into my training today?' 'What can I learn today that will help me towards my goals?'

And last thing at night, ask yourself: 'What did I learn today?' 'What can I do tomorrow to make sure I do even better?' Your unconscious will be working on these questions overnight and, if you're lucky, the answer might be there when you wake up in the morning. Sometimes when you do this, to quote Thomas Edison, 'the answer just dawns on you'.

The following are some examples of empowering questions:

- What can I learn from this situation?
- What am I capable of that I'm not doing yet?
- What do I need to do now to get the result I want?
- What am I happy about at this moment?
- How can I overturn this scoreline?
- What efforts am I willing to make to do better next time?
- How can I have fun while I'm doing it?

Learning to ask the right questions when you're under pressure takes practice but, once you've mastered it, you'll be able to change your emotional state very rapidly. There's no more important skill in sport than this.

Creative Imagery – Your Secret Weapon

I never hit a shot without having a sharp picture of it in my head. Firstly, I see where I want the ball to finish. Then I 'see' it going there, its trajectory and landing. The next scene shows me making the swing that will turn the previous images into reality.

Jack Nicklaus, former international golfer

Colonel George Hall made one of the most incredible comebacks in golfing history when he shot a 76 in the New Orleans Pro-Am Tournament in the early 1970s. Now you may be thinking: 'Seventy-six? That's not a particularly good score, why was it so incredible?' Well, first of all, it was the same score as he'd made in his last tournament 7 years earlier. Secondly, he'd spent 5½ of the intervening years in solitary confinement in a prisoner-of-war camp in North Vietnam.

Every day, he would practise golf in his tiny cell. Not physically, but in his mind. He imagined himself selecting his club, teeing off, driving down the fairway, studying the contours of the green, removing the flag and putting. He played hundreds of holes on dozens of courses, including many he'd only ever seen on television. He rehearsed every shot and replayed every game hundreds of times in his imagination.

After his comeback, a journalist asked him if his success could be attributed to luck. After all, a few short weeks earlier he'd still been languishing in his cell, weak from malnutrition. Colonel Hall smiled, wryly. 'Luck? You must be joking. I never three-putted a green in all my five and a half years of practice.'

Colonel Hall's story shows what can be done using the power of creative imagery. Many winning athletes mentally rehearse their performance over and over again. Most champions could quite easily perform their entire routines blindfolded because they've practised their routines mentally so many times that, by the time they come to do it for real, they've created a solid habit of excellence in thought, word and deed. Whatever the sport – weightlifting, basketball, cricket, archery, skiing, and so on – creative imagery has a vital role to play. If you can learn to do it right in your mind, you can get it right on the day. Get it wrong and you're handicapping yourself, as David Hemery, the 1968 Olympic 400-metres hurdles champion, learned to his cost.

When he won the gold medal in Mexico City, a reporter asked him whether it felt strange running in an Olympic final. 'Not at all,' he replied. 'I expected to win. I had rehearsed the race so many times in my mind, I knew every step I was going to take, so it was easy'. He went on to describe how he had visualized himself running in every lane, because he didn't know in which one he would be drawn. His mental preparation had reduced the risk of being caught unawares.

However, it was a different story 4 years later in Munich. Before the final, he admitted to a journalist that he didn't think he could win. He had visualized himself winning a medal but it wasn't the gold. As it turned out, he won only the bronze. Later, Hemery expressed his disappointment. During the race he'd realized, too late, that he could have actually won if he'd been properly mentally prepared.

Ask any successful athlete and he or she will tell you that the mental training is equally as important as the physical. One of Rex's early clients found this out for himself. George Northcote was a first-division footballer who'd had an accident in a swimming pool. He dived off the high board and landed on someone's head. When he arrived at Rex's consulting rooms he was wearing a neck brace. Needless to say, Rex doesn't miss an opportunity to discuss football, especially when he has a professional prostrate on his treatment table, and he told him about another player who'd visualized himself scoring hundreds of goals. George was intrigued, so he asked Rex to teach him how to do the same.

Rex fixed up his injury and taught him the basics. As George applied them, he began to score more goals. Although his team was almost relegated, he finished as the league's leading scorer for the season. He was so impressed, he started using it in other areas of his life too. He visualized himself gaining a degree at university (which he later did), learning a foreign language and going into business.

At 38 years old, Northcote was a millionaire, still playing first-division football and at the head of a successful business.

Creative imagery works because the unconscious mind (fed from the right brain) finds it easier to accept pictures than words. In addition, the unconscious doesn't have the ability to distinguish between input from the imagination and from the five senses. Think what a powerful tool this is! Your unconscious will believe that you are capable of whatever you can picture yourself doing. This is why athletes like David Hemery report feelings of *déjà vu* when taking part in events which they have mentally rehearsed but never actually experienced before.

When applied steadily, mental rehearsal greatly enhances your chances of success in any endeavour. And scientists have found that mental images even influence your physical body. A few years ago, international sprinters were tested using sophisticated biofeedback equipment which recorded what was happening within their bodies. First, they competed against each other on the track while their muscle activity was carefully measured. Next, they visualized themselves running the race. When the results were analysed, even the scientists were amazed. They showed that the identical muscles were expanding and contracting in exactly the same order when the sprinters mentally rehearsed as when they were running on the track!

The implications of this experiment are clear. Practising in your mind can be as effective as doing it for real! It exercises your muscles and reduces the need for physical training, without incurring the risk of burn-out or injury. When the big day comes the experience is not new (because your mind believes you've been through it all before). The secret is to combine your physical and mental training into a cohesive and balanced programme.

The key to successful creative imagery is to do it *with emotion*. The more you can summon up all the sights, sounds, smells and feelings connected with the experience, the greater the chance of it imprinting on your unconscious. The more realistic you make it, the more your central nervous system responds as if it *is* real.

One way to stir up the emotions and feelings you want is to combine your mental imagery with autosuggestion, which means telling yourself, silently or out loud, that you are unbeatable, determined, or whatever you think would help. Repeat your affirmations and hold the images in your mind until you feel your emotions crystallizing. Then you know you're on your way.

/ Creative imagery techniques

We're going to give you five specific creative imagery techniques to help you improve your chances of winning. If you want to achieve your full potential you must, of course, practise, but this is the kind of practice you will really enjoy. What could be more rewarding than watching yourself performing at your best and winning over and over again!

Five ways to use creative imagery

1 Developing the qualities and abilities you need.
2 Mental rehearsal.
3 Anchoring – accessing peak performance state whenever you want.
4 Re-framing – dealing with past mistakes and defeat.
5 Recovery and relaxation.

1 Developing the qualities and abilities you need

It's only common sense that, to succeed at anything, you must have the right personal qualities and abilities, which means working at them until they become habitual. Many athletes know that if they act 'as if' they already have those qualities, they will become a part of them. Shakespeare put it in a nutshell when he wrote: 'Assume a virtue if you have it not'. So if you do not feel passionate or confident, pretend that you do and, in a few minutes, you will feel that way. But acting 'as if' is not enough. As long as you're 'acting', it's not yet ingrained into you at a deep enough level. Creative imagery can speed up the process of cementing it firmly in place.

Start by deciding which qualities you want. If you've done the exercise in Chapter 2, you'll already know what these are. Work on one at a time at first, until you've got the idea.

Let's say you choose 'courage'. Relax your body (using one of the techniques described in Chapter 10) and begin. Close your eyes and imagine you have a screen, like a cinema screen, on the inside of your forehead. Conjure up an image of yourself behaving courageously. If you are a rugby player, see yourself running for the line, holding off tackles and scoring a try. If you are an ice skater, see yourself doing a breathtaking double spin or flying around in a perfect combination of grace and daring. If you are a boxer, observe yourself fearlessly taking on your opponent. If you are a cricketer, see yourself in control at the crease as a fast bowler runs in and watch yourself coolly hitting the ball to the boundary.

Make the picture a close-up – as big and bright as you can, in full colour, right in the centre of your mental screen. This way, it will have more impact. You probably wouldn't pay much attention to a small, faint, black-and-white image in the corner of your television screen, would you, compared with what's going on in the centre? It's just the same with creative imagery. Practise using your mental screen as often as you can until it becomes very real to you, then move on to the next stage.

Watching yourself compete is a good way of telling your unconscious where you want to go but it has a serious drawback: it's hard to summon up winning emotions because you feel rather detached from the action, just as a spectator in the stands is unable to influence what's going on in the arena. You'll recall (see page 69) that weightlifter Charles Garfield was instructed to imagine watching himself making a lift until this image was firmly fixed in his mind. Do you remember what happened next? It was to imagine himself *actually doing it*. This is your next step, too.

Take yourself back to your chosen image and now imagine the scene as if you were seeing it through your own eyes when in action. What you've done is moved from a *dissociated* position to an *associated* one, which means that you are no longer a spectator but right in the thick of it. Now it's much easier to experience those positive emotions. As you visualize, use affirmations. Tell yourself that you *are* courageous. Really *feel* it and take note of how your body is reacting. Perhaps your pulse has speeded up slightly or your palms are a little sweaty. This is perfectly normal; in fact, it's a good sign because it means that your creative imagery is really working.

2 Mental rehearsal

You are probably already very good at mental rehearsal but you may be using it ineffectively and damaging your prospects if you are using it incorrectly. As we've explained, whatever you hold in your mind has a tendency to manifest itself as reality so, if you are worried or fearful and constantly picture yourself failing, this is exactly what will happen to you. This is why you must master the vital skill of picturing the event exactly as you would like it to turn out.

There are two ways you can use mental rehearsal. The first is to see yourself having already achieved your goal. For example, imagine standing on the rostrum with the medal around your neck or see yourself lifting the cup high above your head. Acknowledge the cheers of the crowd and feel a terrific sense of pride in your achievement. If you are a tennis player, you could watch yourself clearing the net in one victorious leap. Ski jumpers could see themselves gliding to a halt at the bottom of the slope. Get the idea? If you can imagine your ultimate success, you are sending a strong signal to your unconscious that this is what you want and increasing your chances of getting it.

The second use of mental rehearsal is to fix your entire routine firmly in your mind in advance. This is probably the most useful application of the technique. Do it over and over again until it is imprinted on your brain. The more detail, the better. Imagine the exact conditions you will face. What can you hear, see, feel and smell? How warm or cool is it? Can you feel a slight breeze, or the sweat dripping from your brow? Get (or *associate*) into the experience as fully as you can, bringing the image as close and making it as clear as possible. If you're a runner, imagine what it feels like to be a few metres from the end of an Olympic final, knowing you're about to win. Or, if you play tennis, facing the match point that will make you the club champion.

You can use this method to anticipate and deal with possible problems, such as a partisan crowd or unfavourable weather conditions or hard ground. Did you know that Soviet teams were once so unpopular in the West that they used to rehearse mentally to the sound of boos and jeers from an imaginary crowd? Their coaches thought it important to prepare them for a hostile reception whenever they travelled abroad.

Remember, practice makes permanent, so you must continually visualize yourself as you want to be. Be constantly on your guard against programming bad habits into yourself. Do your homework thoroughly beforehand so you are quite certain how you need to perform, then imagine yourself doing it repeatedly. Remember, repetition is the key to learning.

3 Anchoring – accessing peak performance state whenever you want

If you have ever played a perfect shot, you don't need to learn how to do it afresh, you already know. It's conditioned into your unconscious. All you need to do is access that learning and you can play a perfect shot whenever you want. The technique is called *anchoring* and it is one of the most useful weapons in the sporting armoury. So what exactly is anchoring?

Whenever David sees old films of George Best in his prime, he is overwhelmed by feelings of pleasure and nostalgia. His brain has learned to associate pleasure with those images. On the other hand, footage of the Munich air disaster of 1958 has the opposite effect; these pictures can quite easily make him feel sad and miserable. How can this be? These events took place 30 to 40 years ago and, in the case of the Munich disaster, when he was only a small boy.

The fact is, all of us are continually creating associations in our minds which become anchored in our nervous systems. Some of them make us feel good, others leave us feeling drained and depressed. When we see, hear or feel certain stimuli, we react automatically. Think about it. Are there pieces of music which you associate with certain happy events in your life so that, whenever you hear them, the memories and emotions come flooding back? But it's not the music that made you happy *originally*; you've just come to associate it so closely with the emotions you experienced at the time that you can't help yourself feeling good on hearing it.

Seven steps to creating or installing anchors

As we said in Chapter 5, these associations are *anchors* and you can use them to get into the right frame of mind before, during and after a match. Since you already have many anchors, doesn't it make sense to utilize them to help rather than hinder you? Of course it does. We'd like to lead you through a process that enables you to create (or *install*) them in your mind so that they are always available for you. First find a quiet spot where you won't be disturbed, then follow our seven basic steps.

Step 1 Once you are relaxed, take your mind back to your finest hour, when you were really buzzing. (If you can't remember such a time, think of how you would feel if your wildest sporting dreams were to come true.) Experience it fully all over again. How did you look? How did you carry your body? What thoughts flashed through your mind? Picture it all. Imagine you are once again hearing the sounds you heard back then. How did you feel? Re-create those feelings. Associate fully into the situation.

Remember, it's not just the memory you want, it's the emotions which are locked into your unconscious memory banks and your nervous system. Anchoring is all about drawing on your past successes so you can tap into those emotions very quickly any time you want to. One word of warning, though. When you are creating a new anchor or reinforcing an existing one, don't allow your thoughts to wander or you might inadvertently anchor the wrong feeling.

Step 2 When you are experiencing the peak state as intensely as you can, anchor it. This is done by choosing a unique verbal or physical trigger which will send an unmistakable signal to your brain that 'this is it'. We gave you some suggestions in Chapter 5, such as clenching your fists and shouting 'yes'. Other possibilities include phrases such as 'go, go, go' or any others that you wouldn't normally use in everyday speech. In this way, it will be impossible to trigger the anchor by mistake, for example before you are ready or when you want to relax after a match. Alternatively, you could choose an unusual gesture, such as thumping yourself on the chest like an ape or pinching your arm. The best triggers contain a combination of sight, sound and touch, such as repeating a short phrase as you watch yourself beating your chest.

A note of caution is due here. It's extremely important to judge the right moment to fix the anchor precisely. Wait until the feeling peaks. Too soon or too late and you'll anchor a less intense feeling than you could, in which case you'll have to start all over again.

Step 3 Now relax and think of something else. Try reciting your telephone number backwards several times. Then let your mind wander and drift. Allow any tightness and tension to leave your body. When you are thoroughly relaxed once more, go to . . .

Step 4 'Fire' your new anchor by repeating the sequence of sights, sounds and sensations you've chosen, exactly as you did before. Now notice very carefully what is happening. Have those empowering emotions come flooding back? Do you feel confident, courageous, energized? Associate into it. If so, well done, you now have a powerful secret weapon up your sleeve! If not, go back to Step 1 – you haven't quite managed to install your anchor properly yet.

Step 5 Once again, relax, think of something else and let your mind drift. Then, when you are thoroughly relaxed again, go to . . .

Step 6 Project your mind to a coming event, such as an important match a few days away. Visualize it. Mentally rehearse it. When you get to a point where you need an additional burst of energy or that extra touch of confidence, fire the anchor. Immediately see the match going your way. Here's an example.

Imagine you are in the last set of a tennis match and beginning to feel very tired. Conjure up the images, sounds and sensations; and then fire the anchor. Now feel yourself re-energized, serving and volleying with more power and hitting your ground strokes more effectively than before, heading towards a deserved victory. This will strengthen and reinforce your anchor, ready for use when the big moment arrives.

Step 7 On the big day, use your anchor as often as you need, such as when things aren't going too well and you need a boost. Another word of warning, though. If you use your anchor too frequently to help you out of tough situations, you may inadvertently come to associate it with problems and difficulties rather than the surge of energy and confidence you desire, so you must strengthen your anchor by going through our seven-step process often. Remember, 'use it or lose it'. Without frequent reinforcement, an anchor can fade, so take the time to practise using this valuable tool.

4   Re-framing – dealing with past mistakes and defeat

Whether you win or lose, play well or badly, the experience will be wasted unless you learn from it for the future. Jack Nicklaus once summed this up perfectly. On playing his first over-50s' tournament, he said: 'Maybe I'll play well today. Maybe I'll win. Maybe I won't play well and won't win. But whatever happens, I'll learn something from it.'

But, just as you replay your successes in your mind, you can replay your mistakes, but with one big difference. You *correct* them as you go along and play the scene the way you would have liked it to be. This way, you wipe over the old tapes and replace them with new, positive material. The technical name for this process is *re-framing*. It's quite simple but it does take practice. Like all creative imagery, it is best accomplished when you are physically and mentally relaxed. It works in the following way.

If a past event still bothers you, take your mind back and run through it on your mental screen. Then run through it again, only this time seeing it as you would have liked it to have happened, culminating in the outcome you would have chosen. As with the other creative imagery techniques, conjure up all the sights, sounds, smells and feelings you associate with the event, make the picture big and bright, and hold it in your mind for several minutes. Affirm to yourself that this is really happening.

Here's an example to help you. Last year, a local 1,500-metres runner,

Maggie Handley, was overtaken on the last bend after being in the lead for most of the race. She eventually came third. This defeat had weighed heavy on her mind, undermining her confidence. She wondered if she had enough stamina ever to win a big race.

Her trainer realized that this experience was likely to damage her career unless it was properly dealt with, so he had her relax and run through the race in her mind – with a difference. Once again, Maggie was back on the track, heading the field towards the last bend, seeing first one runner then another overtake her and beat her to the line. Then he talked her through the closing stages of the race again, only this time, when the first runner tried to pass her, she felt a new lease of life and was able to hold her off. She saw the scene big and bright, was able to imagine hearing the cheers of her friends and feel the slight breeze on her face as she powered her way forward, shoulder to shoulder with her rival. Then, in the last few metres, she felt a tremendous surge of energy and opened up a sizeable gap. As she imagined crossing the line, she was overwhelmed with relief and exhilaration. She'd done it!

Repeated practice will erase the old feelings of disappointment and replace them with a new-found confidence. Remember, the past does not equate with the future. Whether you won or lost last time has little bearing on the next race, unless you allow it to. This is where re-framing comes in. It reduces the impact of past 'failures' and helps you to learn from them, so your chances of winning next time around are substantially increased.

Sometimes we are asked: 'But, surely, you are just lying to yourself? If you lost, you lost. What's the point of pretending you won when you didn't?' Of course you can't change the past, it's over and done with, but you can change your perception of it. Take Maggie as an example. Because of her past experience, she believed that she couldn't win a 1,500-metres race and this belief would surely have prevented her from performing at her best in future races. Re-framing changed this belief. It sent a new, powerful message to her unconscious. 'You *can* do it. You *do* have what it takes. You have reserves of energy and stamina waiting to be tapped whenever you need them.' Sometimes it is necessary to suspend disbelief when you are practising creative imagery!

5 Recovery and relaxation

Naturally, after the event you'll want to make full use of your recovery time so that you are soon fit and ready for action again. Creative imagery will help you to relax and recover, and ensure that you learn from the day's events.

It is very useful to conduct an 'evening review' of your day last thing at night, just before you drop off to sleep. Go through your day, seeing, hearing and sensing everything working out as you would have wanted. Do this several times. Ask yourself: 'What did I do well?' 'In which areas have

I improved?' 'How could I have done better?' 'What could I have done differently?' This way, whatever you learned during the day will be programmed into your brain ready for use in the weeks and months ahead.

Recovery from injury – a three-step procedure

Another powerful use of creative imagery is to speed up recovery if you have injured yourself. We'd like to offer a three-step procedure that produces excellent results.

Step 1 Relax. Focus on your breath. Imagine it is a form of healing energy (or prana). As you exhale, mentally direct this healing energy to the injured part. Affirm 'My . . . is healed and strong'.

Step 2 Visualize the part as already healed. If it is a cut, see the flesh repaired. If a break, see the bone neatly knitted together. If there is any swelling, see the joint back to its normal size. Don't worry if you're not sure what a broken bone or sprained muscle look like; imagine how it would look and let your unconscious take care of the rest.

Step 3 Visualize yourself doing all the things you will be able to do once you have fully recovered from the injury, with all the energy and enthusiasm you had before. Remember, focus your mind on what you do want, *not* what you don't want, and you will be pleasantly surprised how the healing process can be speeded up.

Creative imagery is truly your secret weapon, since it harnesses the combined power of your physical body and its commander-in-chief – your mind. Everyone can use it, including those who have difficulty actually 'seeing' pictures in their mind's eye. If this is true for you, don't worry; it is not necessary to be able to conjure up a crystal-clear image for it to work well. Some people are more adept at working with sound or touch than vision and, if you are one of these, use whichever sense makes you feel most comfortable. If, for example, you are an 'auditory' type, imagine all the *sounds* that you associate with an event. If you operate better with touch, imagine all the *feelings*. Your brain instinctively knows which way is right for you.

We'd like to finish this important chapter with some valuable hints which will help you get the most out of your creative imagery sessions:

- Mental practice is just as important as physical practice, so allocate time to it *every day*.
- Create a *mental training plan* and stick to it.

- Work out your practice sessions *in advance*. The better you practise, the better the results.

- *Pick a time* when you're normally undisturbed and find it easy to relax.

- Visualize yourself winning. Focus on your goal. *Keep your mind on what you want*, not what you don't want.

- Experience the situation *as if you are actually doing it*, not through the eyes of a spectator.

- *Use all the senses* – sight, hearing, touch, smell and (if possible) taste. Use positive self-talk as you do so.

- Summon up as much *positive emotion* as you can – passion, enthusiasm, confidence, etc. If you find this difficult, start by thinking passionate, confident thoughts and the feeling will come.

- Repetition is the key to any kind of learning, so acquire the skill and *do it over and over again* until you've mastered it. Take small steps at first, then build on them as your confidence grows.

Preparing for the Big Event

*Winning can be defined as the science of being totally
prepared.*

George Allen, England cricketer (1902–89)

Imagine, if you can, the life of a professional boxer preparing for a crucial bout. The rewards may be great but the existence is spartan, the regime punishing. For 6 months, he spends every day in the gym, confined to a training camp, cut off from his family and friends. Endless hours practising punching and footwork skills; weights and stamina training to make the body tough and lean; a stringent diet rigorously enforced. By the day of the big fight, he has reached peak fitness, his mind is calm and focussed. He is totally prepared for the challenge ahead.

In contrast, top teams facing a cup final or an international are usually taken away to a plush hotel for a few days where they can complete their preparation away from the pressure of the public gaze. Here, they can get in tune before facing the battle.

Naturally, you wouldn't hide out in the mountains to train for a local swimming gala or spend a week in the Canary Islands prior to the parents' race at school sports day – your preparation will be related to the size of the challenge you face. But the principle is exactly the same. Quite simply, if you want to be at your best, your body must be in top condition, your skills practised and perfected until they become automatic, your mind and emotions firmly under control.

By now, you already know how to achieve all this, so it's just a question of organizing yourself properly and putting it into practice, which is what this chapter is all about. You probably won't learn anything new but you will be able to make a checklist for yourself which will get you to peak performance at exactly the right moment.

*When I go out there and fight, I become really bad and
determined to beat the daylight out of this guy, because
I don't want him to take away all the hard work,
and if I have to kill him, I will. That's the
attitude I enter the ring with.*

Steve Collins, World Middleweight Boxing Champion

We're going to guide you through the 4 weeks leading up to the eve of a big event so you are at your best when you need to be. Take a leaf out of the Boy Scouts' book and be prepared!

Preparation for the big event

Watch what you eat and drink

Let's begin by reminding you of the importance of a balanced diet, full of nutritious, health-giving foods and rich in minerals and vitamins. This isn't something you should attempt to put right at the last minute – desperate last-ditch efforts are useless here. It's important to adopt a good diet as a way of life so that healthy eating becomes a habit. Remember, you need complex carbohydrates to fill the body's fuel stores with the energy you need and a little protein and fat, together with the right vitamins and minerals, to keep it in good working order. Include plenty of health-giving fruit and vegetables and make sure you are getting enough calcium, iron and magnesium.

To be ready for action, your body's fuel stores must be full of glycogen (starch). After the first few seconds of any exercise, the glycogen stores in your body are mobilized to provide you with energy, then, after a while, you start to utilize your fat reserves and lose some mineral salts through sweating and heavy breathing. So, if you take part in an endurance sport, such as long-distance running or any other event which lasts for more than, say, an hour, you need lots of carbohydrate to prevent or delay exhaustion. Increase your intake of complex carbohydrates for the 2 or 3 days leading up to the event (the term for this is *carbo-loading*), which you can do by filling your plate with wholemeal pasta, brown rice and potatoes and by having at least one banana a day to eat.

If you have followed our advice and taken a multi-vitamin and mineral supplement every day, you needn't worry about losing mineral salts because you'll have plenty in reserve.

As far as your liquid intake is concerned, it's best to drink water little and often to keep fluid levels high. Keep your caffeine and alcohol consumption to a minimum. If you drink alcohol, keep it below the legal driving limit until the last couple of days, when you should avoid it altogether. At the same time, reduce or eliminate your caffeine intake. It's very important to feel calm and relaxed on your big day and too much strong coffee and tea will have precisely the opposite effect.

There are many high-carbohydrate drinks on the market which the manufacturers claim will give you extra energy but we do not recommend them if they contain refined sugars. Refined sugar produces a short-term blood-sugar spike followed by a sudden feeling of weariness – the very last thing you need if you are half way through a marathon! It is far better to drink freshly squeezed fruit and vegetable juices. This way, the natural sugars get into your bloodstream much more quickly, so the energy is both quickly available and longer lasting.

Physical preparation

By now, your body should be in good shape – strong, loads of stamina, muscles and joints loose and supple as a result of the stretching and mobilizing exercises you've done every day, and your aerobic capacity vastly improved. You're fit, full of energy and ready to go. The vehicle is primed, so how are you going to make use of it?

We can't stress enough the importance of practice. You must have all your basic skills so well rehearsed that you don't even have to think about them. You're aiming to get your body and unconscious mind so in tune that your conscious mind can concentrate on more immediate concerns, like executing the tactics you have planned. The secret is simply repetition: doing it correctly over and over again until it becomes a habit.

If you have access to video equipment, you can ask a friend to record you in action. This way, you can study your technique in the comfort of your own living room, see where you are going wrong and decide how to correct it.

By the time the big day arrives, you'll want all the necessary skills to be internalized so that they are an integral part of you. The last thing you need is to have to re-learn a skill a few days beforehand because you've been doing it wrongly. Many professionals have discovered this to their cost. Golfers who have tried to adjust their swing a few days before a major championship have found it almost impossible. Teams who have tried to alter their style of play at the last minute have found themselves floundering on the day. With a little careful planning you can make sure you don't get yourself into this situation.

Of course, you won't want to be training every spare minute as your big day approaches or you'll soon burn yourself out – so make sure you get plenty of rest. Carry out regular relaxation sessions (you'll be doing this as a matter of course if you're doing your mental training because deep physical relaxation is a fundamental part of it). The closer you are to the big match, the stricter you should be about your relaxation sessions.

The human body responds well to regular bedtimes, preferably long before midnight. Players whose sleep is disturbed the night before an event are at a huge disadvantage, so get to bed at a reasonable time. To sleep, of course! There has been much debate about the wisdom of other bed-related activities the night before a match and many coaches enforce strict 'no sex' rules. Some take it even further. For example, a Chinese athlete, Liu Dong, the world 1,500-metres champion, was once dropped from the national team because she refused to give up her boyfriend. And as recently as the 1950s, male British athletes were advised to sleep with a bottle tied to their backs to prevent them from falling into a deep sleep and having a wet dream! Coaches at that time believed that sexual activity sapped male athletes of the hormone testosterone, which makes them more aggressive.

In our view, this was going much too far. After all, the average sex act uses up about the same amount of energy as a 100-metres dash, so most athletes are not likely to harm their chances too much by having sex the night before. A whole night of passion would perhaps have more severe consequences but not because of the sex itself; the lack of sleep would be much more damaging!

For example, in the 1920s, the American World Champion boxer, Harry Greb, had quite a reputation as a ladies' man. After several months training in isolation for a world title fight, he took a fancy to the lift girl in the hotel where he was spending the night before the fight. As he was making his way to his room, he saw her standing in the lift. Quick as a flash, he sprinted across the lobby and slammed the lift door shut. Everyone watched in amazement as the indicator stopped between the sixth and seventh floor. His manager was wailing 'Oh Harry, what have you done?', but his expectations were confounded. The following day, Greb easily retained his title.

Use the modelling technique

The wonders of modern technology have made it easier and easier for top sports people to study the opposition. Every day, television brings us pictures of the important events around the world. We can sit in our own homes in the UK and watch the England–West Indies Test match live from the Caribbean, or the Lions rugby tour of Australia. Italian and American football are beamed directly to our screens, live, every Sunday afternoon. Most people have video-recorders and can record directly from a television signal. There are thousands of excellent sports videos available in the shops and libraries, so anyone can quickly and easily watch the top stars at their best anytime they wish.

Once upon a time, a boxer would have to go and see his opponent live to weigh up his style and his strengths and weaknesses, which made it difficult if he only fought every 6 months or so. Now, he can study him endlessly – forwards, backwards and in slow motion. In cricket, a bowler can study each batsman's technique and memorize his weaknesses (Robin Smith has found this to his cost – every captain he plays against is well aware of his vulnerability to leg spin bowling).

On page 34, we recommended modelling. Remember, you can save yourself years of practice by finding out how someone else does something and then borrowing their approach. The weeks leading up to your big day are a good time to take advantage of this. If you have been able to capture your own performance on videotape, you can easily compare yourself with the best in the business. Be careful who you choose as a model. If you are short and stocky, you don't have the physical attributes needed to play tennis like Ivan Lendl or bowl like Joel Garner; choose someone more appropriate. Observe them carefully. Every little gesture may contribute to them getting into, and remaining in, peak state. A scratch of the side of the nose may just be the anchor your hero or heroine uses to maintain the emotional state they have cultivated for that big occasion.

We're assuming you've already backed up your research by reading books and articles about your role model. Perhaps the last few days leading up to your big challenge are not the best time to start any intense research but you can refresh your memory by briefly going over your reading material to remind yourself of the key points. Many people find it helpful to keep a small notebook to jot down all the ideas and hints they have gleaned.

Now you've a good grasp of how your favourite stars have performed, you may begin to . . .

Study the opposition

In almost every sport, studying your opponents in detail will help you to win. Although amateurs won't be able to go down to their local library and find a video-recording of their next opponents, there are many ways of finding out about them. If you can, go and watch then in action and observe their style at first hand. Make a careful note of what they do well and what they do badly. What about their character and temperament? A highly strung opponent can always be out-psyched by someone with a strong, calm mind. If you play a team sport, study your opponents' tactics, the formation they use and their physical strengths and weaknesses. Do they engage in *gamesmanship*, designed to put their opponents off? If so, be aware of it; we'll return to it in the next chapter.

Ask around. What is their reputation? If possible, talk to someone who has already beaten them and someone who has been beaten by them and find out how they did it. Remember, you are aiming to have a detailed, thorough and objective checklist of all their strengths and weaknesses.

Your next task is to . . .

Decide your tactics

Studies show that the best way to win is to utilize your strengths and skirt around your weaknesses, which means concentrating on what you do well. It's perfectly logical, isn't it? When are you most confident? When you're thinking about your victories or your defeats? It's obvious that we all feel stronger when we have our successes etched clearly in our minds.

Some opponents do have reputations that can bother or even frighten the opposition, in which case you must reinforce your conviction that you can win in every possible way. Vince Lombardi, the legendary American football coach, knew how important this is. He would show his teams films of their opponents giving away vital points and losing. Geoff Boycott provided a wonderful example when he was commentating on an England–West Indies 1-day cricket international in February 1994. A colleague pointed out that the West Indian batsman, Brian Lara, had made a double century, two single centuries and a half century in his last four innings. Boycott shrewdly replied that, by the law of averages, he must be due for a failure!

There's never been a player or team who didn't have weaknesses. Think of the supposedly invincible Leeds United team who lost to Sunderland in the 1973 FA Cup final, or the Soviet ice hockey team losing to the USA in the 1980 Winter Olympics. The history books are full of countless examples of underdogs exploiting the Achilles heels of their opponents.

Intensify your mental training

Now is the time to step up your mental training. Begin by firmly taking charge of your thinking; If you haven't done so already, place yourself on the seven-day mental diet (page 83). Banish all thoughts of failure or defeat. Don't allow yourself to dwell on problems, instead focus on how you are going to overcome them. Carefully construct your affirmations using the five Ps (page 84). Recite them over and over again, using deep breathing and mirrorwork to add to their power. Make a list of all the reasons why you *can* win, drawing on all your past experiences, and why you *should* and *must* win, so that the idea of losing seems much too painful even to contemplate.

Constantly practise taking control of your emotions in everyday situations. Use your physiology, focus your attention on the positive aspects of situations, learn to be 'in the moment' and concentrate totally on whatever you're doing at the time. The more you use these skills when you're away from the sports arena, the more effective they'll be when you really need to use them.

If you feel under immense pressure, here is a useful technique. It will make you realize that, whatever happens, you will always live to fight another day. Relax completely and then think of the worst possible thing that could ever happen to you in sport. Let's say your biggest nightmare would be losing in the first round to a player who you really should beat very easily. How bad would it be? The shame! The embarrassment! The loss of confidence!

Now take your mind forward 6 months. How do you feel? You probably still remember the defeat but it won't seem nearly as disastrous. You've won quite a few matches since then and the worst of the pain will be long gone. Now go forward to one year ahead. By now, you've almost forgotten it altogether. Two years on and it's gone completely. Your worst possible scenario has turned out to be far from the calamity you had thought it was.

If you've followed our advice, you'll have become quite skilled at noticing the kind of words you use as you go about your daily activities. You'll appreciate the advantages of using only words that empower. You'll also have got into the habit of asking yourself empowering questions which trigger constructive responses in your brain. You need to have ingrained the habit of using positive self-talk (page 92) deep into your psyche so you respond automatically to every event with a positive thought. From the moment you wake up in the morning, harness the power of positive thinking.

Hypnosis

Prior to losing his World Middleweight Boxing title to Steve Collins in 1995, Chris Eubank tried to have the bout called off on the grounds that Collins had cheated by consulting a professional hypnotist. Collins was not alone; Frank Bruno and Nigel Benn did so too before winning world titles.

Cricketer Robin Smith also sought the help of a hypnotist after being almost blinded by a delivery from a West Indian fast bowler. 'We practise batting and fielding a lot,' he commented, 'but at least half of the game is played in the head and that part is neglected.' Smith was able to regain his place in the England cricket team on the winter tour of South Africa in 1995.

Hypnotism is often controversial but what are the facts? Hypnosis is simply a state of very deep relaxation. In fact, you've read about it under a different name – alpha level (page 74). As you know, when the mind and body are deeply relaxed, you are able to communicate directly with the unconscious part of the mind. It is probably *the* most effective way of building the all-important confidence and self-belief. David recently used hypnosis to help a European silver medallist rebuild his confidence for the kick-boxing world championships after a period of illness had interrupted his training and to help a former rowing champion recover from a serious back injury.

A professional hypnotist will certainly help you to relax, to become more confident, to eliminate negative thoughts and emotions and mentally rehearse effectively, but you don't have to go to the expense – you can do it for yourself. In Chapter 10, you have all the information you need. Alternatively, you can use a relaxation tape such as *Relax and Decide To Win* (see page 142).

Use your creative imagery

Once you have your thinking right, bring on the heavy guns in your psychological armoury – re-framing, mental rehearsal and anchoring.

Re-framing

Perhaps you still have some negative material in your mind which will block your path. Are you (still) carrying painful memories of defeat or a nightmare practice session when nothing seemed to go right? Re-frame it.

You can do this in two ways. If there was a special reason for the fiasco, remind yourself of what would have happened if circumstances had been different. If you had just returned after injury or illness, affirm that this time you will be fully fit and raring to go. Alternatively, run the event through in your mind, only give it a different ending. Tell your brain how you would have liked it to turn out. Back it up with solid evidence of why it should, and could, have happened like that. This way, if the situation ever recurs, you will instinctively know how to handle it better.

Mental rehearsal

As the big day approaches, mental rehearsal assumes a new importance. Until now, it has probably been rather vague, since you weren't yet sure who you were competing against or under what conditions. But now it's becoming clearer, so incorporate this information into your creative imagery. See yourself executing your carefully planned tactics. If you anticipate facing specific problems, perfect your strategy in your mind. Far better to iron out any problems at this stage than once the contest begins!

Always be aware of your feelings when you rehearse the match in your imagination. Don't forget to focus your attention on the emotions which will place you in a positive, high-energy frame of mind. As we've said, unless you intensify these empowering feelings, your mental rehearsal will be less effective than it could and should be.

Bob Hopper was a champion swimmer in his student days. In fact, he only lost a handful of races in his entire career. One day a friend asked him why he was so good. Hopper thought about it for a moment, then replied:

'For several reasons. First, I keep in good shape. Second, I've been swimming since I was two, so I've had lots of practice. I work out hard, never miss a day. I eat the right kind of food. I don't stay up late. You could say I take very good care of myself.

'However, what makes the difference is my mental preparation. I win

113

because in my own mind, I see myself as a winner. Every week, I run the following movie through in my mind: I visualize myself walking into the stadium, smell the chlorine, sense the people watching from the stands, see the light reflected on the water and feel the butterflies in my stomach. I watch myself walking up to the starting blocks, my competitors alongside me.

'I hear everything going very quiet. The starter says: "Swimmers, take your marks". Then I hear the gun going off and I dive into the water. I take the first stroke, pull through, then again. I take a small lead, then, towards the end, the lead widens, I start to feel tired. I gather myself, and with one last burst of energy, forge ahead and win the race. I run the movie through thirty to forty times. When it is time for action, I know what I have to do and I go out and do it.'

Anchoring

It's vital to be able to call on winning feelings whenever you perform, so make sure that you've taken care to develop and reinforce your anchors. The weeks leading up to a big event are a good time to get them properly installed (see page 100) and here are two ways of doing it.

The first is to relax and mentally take yourself back to your finest hour, as described on page 100. We've nearly all had moments like this; just thinking about them gives us energy and makes us feel more confident. Imagine it over and over again. Fix the image so firmly in your head that you can call on it whenever you want. Run it through in slow motion so that you can intensify the emotions and really feel the changes taking place in your body. When those winning emotions are at their peak, anchor them using the gestures and sounds you've chosen.

The second way is to install your anchor when you're playing at your best. This is a more powerful way than simply visualizing; your mind and body are already doing it, so you don't have to call on your imagination at all. The emotions that come to the surface at times like this are exactly the ones you want to anchor – the peak performance state itself!

The evening before

So here you are the evening before your big day. Apart from a few loosening-up exercises tomorrow, all your physical training is done. Now is the time to relax and take it easy. From time to time, you'll read wild stories of famous sportsmen (it usually is men) who go out on the town the night before a big match, have a few drinks and live it up until the early hours but this is emphatically not to be recommended. If you want to do well, you have to be at your best, which means calming and clearing your mind and getting to bed at a reasonable time.

Make your last-minute preparations, such as organizing your equipment and clothing and carrying out your final mental rehearsal, strengthening your anchors and running through your tactics in your mind, making sure you focus on the result you want. Now, once you've done all this, there's only one more thing you have to do – get out there and win!

Today's the Day!

Live in the present moment. Life is a journey to be enjoyed,
not a struggle to be endured.

Dynamic Living Principle No. 8

Rrrinnng!!! Rrrinnng!!! The start of your morning ritual. Reluctantly you open your eyes and glare at the offending clock. 'Oh, drat! It's time to get up. If only I could stay in bed a bit longer. No, I mustn't, it's the big match this afternoon and I've got a lot to do. I'll grab some breakfast (toast and coffee with two sugars) and get on with it. Why am I always so busy? I know I'll forget something. Damn it, I haven't ironed my kit yet and I still need to find out how to get to the ground. Where did I put that map? Oh hell. Why do these things always happen to me?'

On the way to the match. 'I'm starving [stops off and grabs a double burger and French fries swamped in tomato ketchup] and I'm dying of thirst. Better get a large cola as well.'

You arrive at the ground feeling tense and change hurriedly. You catch a glimpse of your opponent looking eager and fresh. 'Oh, heavens, he looks good, I'll never beat him.' What a contrast to the way you're feeling!

In the first few minutes of the match, you have a chance to take the lead but you fluff it. You become dispirited and angry and your performance deteriorates. You lose, without ever showing what you're capable of.

Now, some hours later, you're at home, sinking a few beers, having snapped at your partner and kicked the dog. Tomorrow you'll probably wake up with a hangover. Your big day has gone sour.

What a disaster! And the sad part is, it needn't have been this way. With a little forethought, it could have turned out quite differently. So let's start again. Let's make sure your day ends happily with a satisfying victory rather than the dull thud of an aching head.

How to get it right

The alarm rings. The start of . . .

The first hour

The first hour is the rudder of the day.

Henry Ward Beecher, American clergyman
and writer (1813–78)

Human beings are largely creatures of habit, so you already go through quite a few rituals every morning. You visit the bathroom, get dressed, make yourself a drink and read the newspaper – but these aren't all. Your mind, too, goes through a series of rituals from the moment you wake up and you need to be aware of them because the first hour sets the tone for the rest of the day. At this time, your unconscious mind is at its most suggestible, so it's important that the suggestions you feed in are positive. So start right away, even before you get out of bed, by taking a few deep breaths, reminding yourself of today's goal and forming a clear mental image of yourself having achieved it. Then jump out of bed with enthusiasm, stand in front of a mirror and proudly declare 'I feel terrific', 'I am strong and unstoppable', or any other affirmations which make you feel particularly good. In that first hour, steep yourself in inspirational material (such as motivational tapes, books or magazines) which will help you get into a positive frame of mind. Then you'll find it easier to stay that way for the rest of the day.

Breakfast

On match day you need to avoid heavy meals altogether because they are digested very slowly and make you sleepy. If you've followed our advice, you'll have provided your fuel stores with the energy you will need by carbo-loading during the last 2 or 3 days, so today you can eat small amounts every couple of hours, starting with fruit for breakfast, a wholegrain mid-morning snack and a light meal at mid-day. These are easily digested and quickly make energy available to you. Whatever you do, avoid anything which contains refined starch or sugar because these will clog your digestive system and eventually drain your energy.

Remember, the fastest way to get nutrients and natural sugars into your bloodstream is to drink freshly squeezed fruit or vegetable juice, so enjoy several glasses between your main meals and top up your fluid intake with natural spring water or herbal teas between meals. If at any time you feel like a snack, eat fruit.

Until a few moments before the match begins, your aim is to remain in the resting state, which means feeling relaxed and drawing on positive emotions.

Now you've had breakfast, this is a good time to put the finishing touches to your . . .

Mental rehearsal

The 20 or 30 minutes you spend using your new-found mental skills today could be the best investment of time you ever make. Why? Because you are programming your mind for success. If you've followed our advice, you'll be very good at this by now – but how can you gain the maximum benefits at this eleventh hour? The most effective way is to go through your entire performance on your mental screen, involving all five senses as much as you can. Don't forget to see yourself as a winner, confident and strong, leaving no doubts that you *can* and *are going to* win. At the same time, review your tactics and imagine yourself executing them perfectly. Whatever your opponent throws at you, see yourself rising to the occasion.

On the way to the match, carry on listening to motivational tapes or reading inspiring stories to keep you in the right frame of mind. You're already well into your . . .

Pre-match rituals

Rituals are important. Successful athletes are well aware of rituals. Some, for instance, put certain items of clothing on in exactly the same order every time; altering their routine would leave them feeling anxious and detract from their performance. For example, a boxer paces around the changing room, stabbing at the air, practising his punches with the trainer. Appropriate rituals relieve tension, build concentration and act as a countdown to peak performance. One of the most important pre-match rituals is, of course, the warm-up routine, stretching and mobilizing the joints so that the body is ready for action.

As you're waiting for the game to start, you'll find all sorts of thoughts popping into your head. Questions such as: 'Have I trained hard enough?' 'How good is my opponent anyway?' 'Do I have enough energy?' 'Am I sure of my tactics?' Use what you've learned from Chapters 10–12 to keep your thoughts positive and try re-phrasing the questions so that they empower you. How about: 'How can I show my opponent I've trained harder than he has?'

The minutes leading up to the kick-off can seem a very long time if you're not properly mentally prepared for them, so design some rituals for calming your nerves and bring the full force of positive self-talk and creative imagery to bear. Do several minutes of deep, diaphragmatic breathing followed by the reciting of your favourite affirmations (such as 'Today is my day. I am at my best') and a visualization of your desired outcome – victory!

One more thing you should consider carefully before you do battle is your appearance. Looking good is closely related to feeling good, so make sure that your clothing and your equipment are conducive to playing as well as you possibly can.

Walking out

When the time comes to walk into the arena, move confidently, demonstrating your power to the opposition. In team sports, emerging on to the field of play can be an important ritual in itself. Players often walk out in exactly the same order: each will have his own particular position – first, second, third, or last, etc. – and no one would feel right if they swapped around.

This might be the first opportunity you have to out-psych your opponent, so make the most of it (we'll return to this on page 123). You shouldn't worry if you're feeling a little nervous, even the stars experience an unsettled feeling in the stomach just before a contest. As we said on page 92, you'll find this much easier simply by changing the words you use to describe it. If you can think of this feeling as 'excitement' or 'anticipation' rather than 'nervousness' or 'fear' it will spur you into action.

Once you're out on the field, you should try to make every action count, so that you stay in the right frame of mind. The All Blacks have a ritual all of their own to get them in the right emotional state. They gesture and chant aggressively in the centre of the field – it puts many opposing teams at a disadvantage even before kick-off! But the warm-up ritual doesn't have to be so dramatic to be effective. Watch a footballer bending and stretching, adjusting his bootlaces and taking a few measured shots at goal; or a runner, pacing up and down, loosening up, staring at the finishing line; or a boxer, tensing his muscles and dancing around the ring.

I give him a look one last time before the fight starts.
I close my eyes and go right through my build-up, from the
time I started, as far back as I can remember, and bring
myself to this point, and think: 'I'm ready. If I can't do
it now, then I'm not the best.'

Steve Collins, World Middleweight Boxing Champion

One performer who has stuck in Rex's mind is the South African tennis player, Kevin Curran, who played Boris Becker in the 1985 Wimbledon men's final. Although he was seeded and favourite to win, when he walked on to the court his head and shoulders were down, he looked anxious and over-awed by the occasion. In contrast, the 17-year-old Becker had nothing to lose – he'd already confounded everyone's expectations by reaching the final. Curran put up little resistance as Becker powered his way to victory – the only unseeded player (and the youngest) ever to win the championship.

The match

Once the game begins there are some skills you just can't afford to be without. For instance, you must be able to summon up all the energy you need, concentrate and stay in tune during the time between points or lulls in the action. You must be able to overcome mistakes and accept unfair decisions from match officials without letting them upset you. You must also be able to cope with gamesmanship (page 123) from your opponents and, if you choose, execute some ploys of your own.

We're going to take a look at each of these in turn, using ideas and techniques we've already presented to you in previous chapters. Once you've learned to bring them all together, you'll be in a very powerful position to beat even the most challenging rival.

I Managing your energy level and your emotions

Cast your mind back to Chapter 5 and you'll recall how important it is to be able to switch rapidly from low energy to high energy, and back again at will. In Chapter 11, we expanded on this and described some of the ways people react to pressure. Perhaps they felt uncomfortably familiar to you!

The best way of coping with pressure is, of course, to use the techniques we've given you to stay confident and positive and enjoy what you're doing. Here, the anchoring technique is a boon – with a little practice you can generate the feelings you want at will. In time, you'll know instinctively when you've slipped from peak state and correct it before any damage is done, whether you're on top or need to come from behind to win.

In addition to managing your energy levels, the other major challenge that you face is . . .

2 Concentration

Maintaining your concentration means being entirely present 'in the moment' and focussing your attention on what you want rather than what you don't want. When your brain is locked on to what you *don't* want, you're making it almost impossible to get what you *do*. Here's an example.

One of the drivers in the Indianapolis 500 was once asked how he managed to hold his nerve when he was overtaking alongside the concrete wall at the edge of the circuit. His reply was very illuminating. 'You concentrate on what you want. If you look at the wall and think "I'd better not hit that wall", you're going to hit it. If you look at the driver you're going past and think about hitting him, the likelihood is you will. What you do is look at the opening, see yourself going through it, and give it all you've got.'

Top golfers play every hole as if it's the first. They shut out anything that has gone before, including mistakes made at the same hole in the previous round. At our local golf club, one of the fairways borders a lake. We've noticed some of the less experienced players switching their best golf balls for well-used ones before teeing off. No doubt they think it's a good precaution in case it goes in the water. Just pause for a moment and think about it. What effect will this action, which (perhaps unconsciously) focusses the attention on the least desirable outcome, have on their play? Well here's a strong clue – every year the club hires a professional diver to retrieve lost balls from the lake and he always fills several large bins!

Let's imagine you are facing a crucial point in the game, such as a penalty kick or a moderately easy shot to pot the black and win the club snooker championship. Here's a routine you can use to sharpen your concentration and put yourself in the right frame of mind. Just before taking the shot, step back and use your relaxation and imagery skills. Take a deep breath, momentarily close your eyes, count down from three to one and visualize yourself achieving what you want to accomplish and doing it perfectly. At the same time, say to yourself 'score! or 'pot!' Then step up and do it for real.

Your concentration, confidence and energy levels are all going to be directly influenced by what you say to yourself, so it's also absolutely vital to keep control over your . . .

Self-talk

Your internal dialogue is likely to speed up and gets even louder when you're under pressure. Sports scientists once wired up leading tennis players to recording equipment and asked them to verbalize everything that was going through their heads. The results were fascinating; they were constantly talking to themselves, affirming that they could do it and reassuring themselves after mistakes had been made. They were using positive self-talk to keep them in peak state.

Self-talk is important, so be prepared. During the contest, you can recite or even sing your favourite affirmations quietly to yourself. Many top athletes hum a tune or repeat a favourite phrase over and over in their minds to keep them sharp. This is well worth trying because it makes you less likely to listen to the small, critical voice within, which could damage your self-confidence just when you need it most. And it's especially important to control your internal dialogue during those moments when the heat is temporarily off, in other words, during the . . .

Down-time

You'll have to cope with down-time in almost every sport, for example, those moments in team games when you're waiting for a set piece to be taken; in cricket or baseball, it's the time when you're waiting to come in and bat, or when you're fielding and not directly involved in the action; in snooker, it's when your opponent is at the table.

If you've learned how to manage it effectively, down-time is a godsend. It is your opportunity to take a breather and re-energize yourself. But if you allow your self-talk to get out of hand, it will defeat you just as surely as anything that happens once you're back in action. Do some deep breathing, relax, keep your thoughts positive and focus on your goal. If you are allowed a given period between points, use every precious second to the best possible advantage. For example, if you play tennis, never rush back on court after the down-time between games until you have to. Your priority is to conserve energy and recover your poise before getting back into the fray.

It's also crucial to be able to avoid discouragement and manage your internal communications when . . .

Handling mistakes

When you've blundered, there's always the temptation to let your self-talk get out of control, blaming yourself and convincing yourself that you've blown it. Top players don't do this, of course. They simply shrug their shoulders, turn and walk away and say to themselves: 'Let it go. No problem. It's OK. I can deal with this.' They use powerful rituals which will enable them to carry on – with their concentration and self-belief undiminished. Rather than asking destructive questions, such as 'Why am I such an idiot?' or 'Why can I never get it right?', they ask 'How can I make sure I get it right next time?' 'How can I improve?' Remember, there is no such thing as failure, only results!

You simply must learn how to wipe a mistake from your memory so it won't chip away at your concentration and leave you discouraged. The best way is to use instant re-framing. When professional golfers miss a shot, for instance, they immediately swing the club as they should have done, while visualizing the ball going where they wanted it to.

In addition to using your new-found mental skills to improve your own game, you may also wish to try and upset your opponent's concentration and confidence. The best way to do this, of course, is to play as well as you possibly can but, depending on your attitude towards it, you may also try to out-psych them using . . .

Gamesmanship

Some of the greatest champions never felt the need to resort to gamesman-ship. They were so good at their chosen sport that all they had to do was play to their own high standards to be sure of winning. One such person was Jack Nicklaus. Once, in the 1969 Ryder Cup, he was playing Tony Jacklin. On the final hole, Jacklin was left to sink a nerve-racking 60-centimetre (2-foot) putt to square the tie. Nicklaus smiled and picked up Jacklin's marker, conceding the putt. Shaking hands, he said: 'I don't think you would have missed, but I was not prepared to give you the chance.' What a sportsman!

However, the reality is that gamesmanship abounds. The master was, of course, John McEnroe who used seemingly childish tantrums to pump himself up and put off his opponents. Despite the ranting and raving, however, his mind never wandered from the task of winning. As we've said earlier (page 88), it wouldn't work for most people but McEnroe was very successful so obviously it achieved the right results for him. Usually, though, games-manship is more discreet, for instance, stopping to tie your bootlace as your opponent is about to take a crucial shot, posing and time-wasting, complaining to umpires and referees, and so on. Sometimes, footballers (and others) are able to get opponents to retaliate, and thus sent off the field, by swearing and spitting at them until they crack.

We aren't condoning such actions, especially if they lie outside the spirit of the rules of the game and destroy the enjoyment for spectators, but, on the other hand, we know that anything you can *legitimately* do to out-psych your opponent before or during the game can bring you enormous advantages. For example, André Agassi frequently stands inside the baseline to receive service during a tight match in an attempt to break his opponent's concentration. In the 1993 Test Series against England, the Australian Captain, Allan Border, immediately called on his leg spinner, Shane Warne, to bowl whenever Robin Smith came to the crease. And in the 1978 World Cup in Argentina, when Scotland was awarded a penalty against Peru, the Peruvian goalkeeper leaned against the right-hand post until the very last moment as a ploy to disturb the Scottish penalty taker – and the shot was saved.

Out-psyching can also take a more subtle form. For instance, on the eve of the last stage of the 1989 Tour de France, the leader, Laurie Fignon, approached the second-placed Greg Lemond. 'Congratulations,' he said, 'you've ridden a great race, and it's exactly as I imagined it would be, me first and you second.' But Lemond was wise to the tactic. He thanked him but inwardly thought to himself: 'I'm not going to let you out-psych me, pal.' Next day, he won the final stage by an incredible 57 seconds to take the winner's yellow jersey for the second time.

Out-psyching your opponent can start weeks before the contest. Muhammad Ali was a master at this. If you have a long memory, you may recall a furious Sonny Liston, completely out of control after Ali had said he was too ugly to be the World Heavyweight Boxing Champion. Ali used similar ploys many times in his career and the results speak for themselves. But you probably won't be able to use the same tactics – after all, Ali had the world's media on his side. So what can you do to win the battle of nerves before and during a game?

The first thing you must do is to make sure that you are physically and mentally in tune, yourself. If you're not, trying to out-psych your opponent will backfire on you. You need plenty of energy and concentration to devote to your own performance and diverting some of this energy to another's game could seriously distract you. So, before you attempt psychological fun and games, make sure you can carry it off without disturbing your own concentration. If not, don't even try. Instead, simply project positive thoughts at your opponent. Since others often pick up our feelings intuitively, directed thoughts, such as 'I'm going to win, you can't do anything to stop me', will find their mark. Imagine you are transmitting a radio message to your opponent.

If you have a physical asset, you can use this to the full advantage. Draw yourself up to your full height. Show off your muscles. In contact sports, jostle and nudge your rival so he feels the full brunt of your physical power.

If you really want to use these kinds of tactics, you can also tell your opponents about your strengths and rub their noses in their weaknesses. As Muhammad Ali's references to Liston's appearance prove, 'truth' is relative, so what you say doesn't necessarily have to be true, or relevant, to achieve the desired result. If you feel so inclined, tell them they have a body odour problem, or are boring, or that the fans hate them and want them to lose.

You must, of course, be prepared for others to use the same against you. If you find yourself on the receiving end, it's important to keep control of yourself and, if you choose to retaliate, do so in a way that is unexpected and will disturb your opponent's concentration – the element of surprise is all-important. But in the words of the old saying, 'If you can't stand the heat, stay out of the kitchen'. Or adopt the approach once used by the late Arthur Ashe when playing the volatile Ilie Nastase. Nastase was on his worst behaviour – cursing, challenging the officials and hurling abuse at his opponent. Finally, even though he was winning, Ashe put down his tennis racket and walked off the court, telling the umpire that he was afraid he'd lose control.

'But Arthur,' the umpire pleaded, 'you'll default the match.'

'I don't care,' replied Ashe. 'I'd rather lose that than my self-respect.'

Next day, the tournament committee met. They knew that they'd be condoning Nastase's behaviour if they disqualified Ashe, which would set a dangerous precedent. They decided instead to disqualify Nastase – a victory for good sportsmanship – and common sense.

However, if you feel you have to resort to bursts of cursing and disruption to win your matches, then you're obviously not good enough to win on your own merits. Perhaps you ought to read through this book again to make sure at least the mental side of your game is in order!

When it's all over

The final whistle has blown, the winning stroke has been played and you now know the result. Did you win? Congratulations. Or did things not work out as you would have wanted? Whatever the result, no doubt you did your best and, now the action's ended, you can get into your post-match ritual. Your body can recuperate, your mind can relax and unwind and you can evaluate your performance and take stock of what you've learned – ready for next time.

The first thing on your mind will be refreshment. Probably you've lost fluid and will be thirsty, so drink plenty of spring water. You'll also need to replenish your fuel stores and it's best to start soon, because it will take a couple of days to re-stock the carbohydrates. Even if you're not feeling hungry, eat fairly soon after exercise, at least a sandwich or a banana to tide you over until your next balanced meal.

As soon as the match finishes, revert to the resting state – if you've installed a specific anchor to help you relax, this is a good time to use it. Later, when you've got 20 or 30 minutes to spare, go into alpha level and carry out your post-match evaluation. Ask the 'voice in your head' to give you feedback and suggestions for next time and use re-framing to clear up any incidents which did not go the way you wanted. It's far more effective to do this when you're relaxing peacefully than when you're in the middle of the action, and the results will be fed deep into your unconscious mind.

Finally, just before you go to sleep, carry out your regular evening review to cement the lessons you have learned firmly in place.

So there you are, one more learning experience along life's path – and hopefully an enjoyable and successful one. If this is the first time you've employed your new mental skills, we hope they've worked well for you and you've achieved what you set out to do – become a winner!

Watch What You Say!

*If you keep on saying things are going to be bad, you have
a good chance of being a prophet.*

Isaac Bashevis Singer, author and winner of Nobel Prize

One Saturday afternoon, shortly after footballer Kevin Keegan had made
it into the first team, Liverpool were playing West Ham. Bill Shankly, the
Liverpool manager, knew that Keegan would probably be marked by Bobby
Moore, the West Ham and England Captain. Facing such a famous player
could be rather daunting for a relative newcomer, so he took Keegan aside in
the dressing room a few minutes before the match. 'I've just seen Bobby
Moore,' he said. 'He's looking very weary. It must be hard for him at his age.
He's obviously over the hill.'

Heartened by his manager's words, Keegan played a blinder, giving Moore
a torrid afternoon. In the changing room after the game, Shankly said to
Keegan: 'Well done, son, you were terrific. And do you realize you've just
outplayed one of the greatest players the world has ever seen?'

No wonder Bill Shankly had the reputation as one of the best motivators in
sport. His wit and cunning were legendary and he could always find a word
or two to encourage and inspire his players and deflate the opposition. But
words aren't always necessary. The other Merseyside giants, Everton, once
faced a difficult away tie in the FA Cup. Everton had been struggling and
badly needed a good cup run to restore their sagging pride. Just before the
match, the Everton manager, Howard Kendall, strode into the changing room
and flung open the windows. The sound of Everton's passionate fans singing
and chanting filled the room. 'That's my team-talk,' said Kendall and walked
out. Fired with determination, Everton won 2–0.

In this book, you've learned a lot about communicating with yourself. Now
we're going to discuss the vital importance of communicating with others.
Good communication skills can make all the difference. Coaches communicate with players, players with team mates, match officials and the opposition.
Spectators often have a lot to say to players and ambitious parents encourage
their children. Of course, words are not the only form of communication:
 research has shown that 55 per cent of the message received is from gestures

and body language, 38 per cent from tone of voice and only 7 per cent from the words themselves. However, a few correctly delivered, well-chosen words can make the difference between success and failure. But how many of us have ever learned to communicate effectively? How many really understand how to express ourselves so that our words have the desired effect? And who better to teach these skills than the psychologists who have studied them for many years?

Until the early 1980s, many players and coaches were quite suspicious of psychologists. Take Bruce Longdon, who coached hurdler Sally Gunnell to an Olympic gold medal in 1992. He encourages other coaches to learn all they can about communication so that they don't have to rely on specialist sports psychologists. We can only agree. Every coach needs to know how to persuade, enthuse and encourage others into doing (sometimes uncomfortable) things. They must know how to develop team spirit and cohesion, tailoring their approach to the individuals in the team. The old-fashioned way was to use fear – shouting and hurling abuse or imposing additional training sessions on the team until they got it right. But this rarely gets the best results. Is it possible to frighten people into doing what you want?

The answer is a guarded 'yes'. If a robber points a gun at your head, you hand over the money, don't you? The problem is that fear leaves you emotionally disabled, even rooted to the ground, which in sport isn't a good thing. What you want is a person with greater energy, greater determination and greater enthusiasm. You certainly won't get that by intimidating people.

Coaches who communicate with their players in a clumsy or overbearing way can inadvertently undermine their motivation, distract them and ruin their concentration. Clearly this is the last thing they would want, yet it frequently happens. The coach's words can, often unknowingly, divert the performer's mind away from what he wants towards what he doesn't want. We say 'unknowingly' because some coaches don't know very much about the working of the mind.

The way the brain works is like this. When you tell someone *not* to do something, the brain must first picture what it is you don't want before it can work out what you do want. It then issues an instruction to do the opposite of what it's been told. Unfortunately, the initial picture (i.e. what you *don't* want) can leave such a firm impression that it swamps the second. Sound's complicated? Not really. Let's give an example.

If a snooker player tells himself 'Don't pot the white ball', his mind, however briefly, sees an image of the white going into the pocket. So where is it likely to go? Since you know the answer we won't dwell on it but we will reiterate, once again, that you should always focus on what you do want, not what you don't want.

127

The same principle works when you're communicating with another person. Negative language can distract them from the desired result and set them up for failure. Just for a moment, imagine you are watching a first-class cricket match. The batsman has scored 99 and looks poised to make a century. The opposing captain wanders over to the bowler to give him some encouragement and some timely advice. 'Don't bowl short down the leg side', he says, 'or he'll hit you for six.' Then he walks back to his fielding position. His words trigger an image-thought in the bowler's mind, 'I mustn't bowl . . .' but too late. He watches the ball being hit out of the ground. The dominant message his brain has picked up are 'short' and 'leg side'. It doesn't make sense to try to motivate someone else by using the opposite of what you really want.

Coaches and captains would do well to bear this in mind. Instead of telling the penalty taker 'Don't shoot to the right or the keeper will save it', tell him to shoot to the left because that's the keeper's weakest side. Instead of saying 'Don't play on his forehand or he'll pass you every time', say 'Concentrate on the backhand, it's a bit fragile'. Not 'Don't let her open up a lead in the early stages or you'll never catch up', but 'Make sure you stay with her for the first 600 metres, so you'll have a good chance of overtaking her when she tires on the final bend'.

A school netball coach once unwittingly set her team up for defeat during the pre-match practice session. 'Missing penalty throws is what loses games,' she said, 'so you're all going to stay behind for an hour to practise them until you stop missing so often.' They lost.

Do you think our approach would have worked better? 'Teams that score from most of their penalty throws win matches. Why don't we spend an extra sixty minutes this week practising penalty shots so that when we get opportunities during our next match, we'll score as many as we can and win the game.'

Using positive language is always much more likely to get you the result you want and you can use this principle at any level, from giving advice about the next shot to be played to setting targets for the whole season. Most people like to have a firm target to aim for so, if you are a coach, don't be frightened to set one and communicate it clearly. Some team talks sound a little like 'Train hard, get out there, take each match as it comes, give it all you've got and play as well as you can, and you'll win matches and do well in the league'. Compare this approach: 'We're going to win the league this year, that's our target, so let's get started.' Which is more likely to inspire your players? Obviously, for most of us, the second.

Be equally sensitive if you use the sort of rousing rituals much beloved of American footballers and rugby players. Some people like lots of cheering and shouting but what about those who prefer to sit quietly just before a match deep in their own thoughts or reading a book? If this is their style, let them get on with it. They'll perform just as well once the game begins.

Which leads us to another important point for coaches working with individuals – if you know what motivates a person, you can use this knowledge to motivate them much more effectively. Some are best motivated by the glory of winning, others by the fear of losing; some by a love for the sport, to be remembered as the best ever, or money. Others simply want to improve every time they play. Always take the individual into account, even in team games.

A sports psychologist working with a team concentrates on developing positive attitudes, in each member, towards him or herself, the team and the performance. Having read this far, you know that there is much you can do to help others improve and succeed. The truth is, no matter how good you are it is a very rare individual who achieves success without at least the cooperation, if not the wholehearted support, of others, whether it be family, friends, coaches or team members.

If yours is a team sport, don't under-estimate the influence of your team mates and the team officials. Would the young Ian Botham, Graham Gooch and David Gower have blossomed as they did at international level without the patient guidance of Mike Brearley, the England Captain, nurturing and encouraging them? We doubt it. Many of the top sports stars owe a considerable debt of gratitude to the older players who taught them by example in the early days of their careers. And this is no more important than the support that parents give to their children, so it is to this that we will now turn.

Encouraging your children

It is never too early to start developing the right attitude in your children because any child who expresses an interest in a given activity can become competent, regardless of natural ability. If your child doesn't appear to have much talent, don't despair – most successful sports stars were not identified as outstanding prospects at an early age and many did not find their true sporting vocation until quite late. For instance, did you know that Sally Gunnell started her athletics career as a long jumper, then a pentathlete, before settling for, and excelling at, hurdling?

We recently heard of a project in Australia that matches youngsters' physical attributes to the sports at which they are most likely to succeed. A computer is used to compare children's physical measurements, such as weight, height, ability to jump and throw, and so on, with the requirements of over 100 sports and activities. The aim is to see which children are most suitable for which sports, so that talent can be spotted at an early age and be developed.

What's wrong with this approach? Can you spot any flaws? Well, firstly, there is no place on this computer for attitudes and mental skills; secondly, there are grave dangers in selecting too early; and thirdly (perhaps most important of all), the child may not enjoy the type of sport that he or she is supposed to 'fit'. Children develop at different rates and any outstanding children may simply be early developers who will lose their advantage as the other children catch up. One striking illustration is given by the England schoolboys football team. Hardly any of these outstanding boys ever become successful professional footballers, let alone full internationals. This is simply because the national youth side is packed with early developers, not future prospects.

We don't agree with the 'factory farming' approach. It is far better to encourage children to take part in a wide range of sports so they develop fit, healthy bodies, positive attitudes and a sense of fun and enjoyment. They can then specialize once they get into their teens, drawing on the range of physical and mental skills they have acquired over the years. Specializing too early can be self-defeating. What if they specialize in the wrong sport and find it hard to change later?

A recent study at the University of Chicago found that most successful children had caring parents who spotted their potential and encouraged their development; parents who taught the virtues of determination, persistence, enthusiasm, patience and practice; who found the time, energy and money for the necessary lessons and equipment; who would think nothing of getting up early three or four times a week to take their children to training sessions and devoting their weekends to taking them to tournaments.

But we feel we must offer some words of caution to parents who think they've discovered a future Wimbledon champion or Olympic gold-medal winner living under their roof. What's your motivation? Are you doing it for your child? Or yourself? Many parents who suffer from low self-esteem want their children to do well to compensate for their own feelings of inadequacy. Your child must *want* to do it, otherwise your efforts will be in vain and you'll be building up a store of future resentment.

We're going to offer six positive actions a parent can take to support a child who wants to excel at sport.

Six positive actions to encourage a child

1   Use praise – not criticism.
2   Don't over-pressurize.
3   Give freely of your time.
4   Find role models.
5   Teach the right mental skills.
6   Help to set goals.

1 Use praise – not criticism

Praise is one of the greatest motivators of all. It take little time and costs nothing, so use it frequently. This doesn't mean, of course, that you should indiscriminately praise everything your child does. This would defeat the object, since there are bound to be things the child needs to improve on and areas where greater efforts are required. The secret is to find something to praise, however badly the child has done, and build up his or her confidence in little things. Avoid negative criticism at all costs; nothing destroys a child's confidence and self-esteem quite so much. Focus on their successes rather than their failures and build on their strengths rather than constantly harping on their weaknesses.

2 Don't over-pressurize

Three years ago, when Dave was at a school sports day, he saw a 7-year-old girl being shouted at by her parents. She had come last in every race she entered. She fell over in the sack race, tripped over the skipping rope and dropped the egg off the spoon, all with a broad grin on her face, obviously enjoying herself. What made it worse was that her Mum and Dad had won the mothers' and fathers' races quite easily; they thought she had let the family down. Sadly, instead of choosing to applaud their daughter for taking part so cheerfully, she was left feeling undervalued just because other children could run faster. This is not the way to encourage your children. They respond best to fun and loving support, not verbal abuse. We would not be surprised if that little girl has been turned off sport for life.

We also knew a man who watched his teenage son play football and who would make quite a spectacle of himself, loudly forcing his opinions on everyone within range. If his son didn't play a blinder, he would criticize everyone concerned – the team coach for playing him in the wrong position, his team mates for not passing him the ball enough, the referee . . . Needless to say, his son was embarrassed, his performances suffered and, because he couldn't persuade his father to keep quiet or stay away, he eventually gave up the game altogether.

3 Give freely of your time

Unfortunately, there are no short cuts here. It can be very time-consuming to take your children to all the training sessions and competitions that are necessary if they are to succeed. Some of them take place at very anti-social times, especially when facilities are limited and required for other purposes during the day. Many swimmers and ice skaters have perfected their art early in the morning or late at night simply because the pool or rink is not available to up-and-coming young people during the day. Sometimes it's hard to be a parent but somehow all the effort seems worthwhile when the results come – not only trophies but children who have more character and a greater sense of purpose than many of their peers.

4 Find role models

Children are great imitators. They need someone to look up to and whose achievements they can aspire to. Most children are naturally drawn towards the national and international teams and heroes they see on television but prominent local heroes can fit the bill just as well. Parents can help by guiding their children towards sports people who have the right qualities and firmly but gently discouraging them from picking up undesirable attitudes and habits from those who set a less wholesome example.

5 Teach the right mental skills

Most children are naturally positive but they do sometimes get discouraged. If you have children, they can benefit from your new-found understanding. You can teach them the importance of the mind and the techniques you have learned, including how to stay positive, overcome defeat, manage their emotions and so on. You can guide them through visualizations: children have good imaginations and take readily to it. Children who learn these skills at an early age are indeed fortunate!

6 Help to set goals

As we've said, goal setting is one of the keys to positive inner motivation. You can help your children set realistic goals, break them down into manageable steps and encourage them along the way. This, too, is a habit that will serve them well in all areas of their life. (It helps if you set an example, of course, by steadily working towards goals of your own.)

Helping your children to do their best in sport is a lengthy process involving physical and emotional support and encouragement, but your efforts will be well worth it. Not only will they do better but you will feel closer to them and develop the kind of warm, loving relationship every parent wants. Moreover, the qualities they build into themselves will serve them well for the rest of their lives.

The Dynamic Formula for Success

Life is a daring adventure – or nothing.

Helen Keller, visually and aurally impaired American writer, lecturer and scholar

What does it feel like to be a winner? Do you know – yet? How badly would you like to know?

Ask any champion and they'll tell you there's nothing quite like it. Your self-esteem rises. You carry your body differently. You feel more alive. You have a clear sense of purpose, so life has meaning for you. Other people respond to you with genuine respect. Above all, your attitude becomes more optimistic and joyful, and your new-found *joie de vivre* impacts on other areas of your life because success at sport carries over into your career, your hobbies, your social life and your spiritual growth.

Should this surprise you? Surely not. If you doubt it, take a look at the list of winning qualities you selected in Chapter 2. If your list was anything like ours, you'll find that the very same attributes are needed whatever you want to succeed at. If you're still not convinced, read through Chapter 3 once again. You can see how our ten-step goal-setting process could help you become anything you want – a business tycoon, an artist, a farmer, a teacher – there really aren't any exceptions.

Now cast your mind back to Chapter 4. Can you think of any activity where it *isn't* necessary to master the basics before going on to more advanced skills? We can't. And doesn't Chapter 5 explain why so many talented young business executives suffer heart attacks at a relatively early age?

They simply haven't learned to switch easily between the intense peak state and the vital resting state, leaving their minds and bodies constantly over-revving like a high-powered engine, in danger of burning out. Champion sports people could certainly teach them a thing or two!

Similarly, following our advice on nutrition, exercise, breathing and mental skills would equip anyone for success at anything. What's the secret? It's really quite simple. It's knowing what you want to achieve, finding out what you need to do and then doing it on a regular basis. It's noticing whether you're getting the results you want and being flexible enough to change course if you're not. Not that hard is it? Providing you keep going long enough, you're bound to get there sooner or later.

What exactly do you need to do to become a winner at sport? How would we sum up the message of this book? Here are 18 points we hope you've gleaned from the last 15 chapters:

- Commit yourself to clear goals.
- Decide to build into yourself the qualities and characteristics of a winner.
- Model the best.
- Practise until you get it right, especially the basics.
- Eat, breathe and exercise correctly.
- Choose winning attitudes and beliefs, and . . .
- Programme them into your unconscious.
- Cultivate a positive mental attitude.
- Take charge of your emotions.
- Be able to trigger the peak state whenever you need to . . .
- And to relax and unwind thoroughly, so you can . . .
- Balance your energy output with adequate recuperation time.
- Learn from your mistakes and setbacks.
- Focus on what you want, not what you don't want.
- Practise and use creative imagery until you've mastered it.
- Act as if you are a winner. 'See' yourself as one.
- Monitor your performance – go for constant small improvements.
- Enjoy it!

The Dynamic Living Formula

If you do all this, how can you fail? And we've developed our *Dynamic Living Formula* to help you get it right. All we ask is that you devote a short time each day to working on your mental training – two sessions of deep relaxation to work at the unconscious level and 15–20 minutes of conscious activity, such as reading self-help books or listening to inspirational tapes. This isn't a great deal of time in relation to the enormous benefits you'll receive. Most people waste at least an hour a day doing nothing in particular but you can invest this time to very good effect.

Dynamic Living Formula

1 Physical relaxation.

2 Mental calmness.

3 Creative imagery.

4 Positive self-talk.

5 The 'as if' principle.

1 Physical relaxation

We couldn't possibly list all the benefits of deep physical relaxation here – there are just too many of them – but they include improved health and vitality, greater resilience to stress and illness, more refreshing and satisfying sleep, improved digestion, and greater mental calm and peace of mind. And this is just the start.

Two 20-minute relaxation sessions a day will enable you to bring about rapid changes in your psyche. The best times are first thing in the morning and early evening before you start feeling tired. Try not to rush your relaxation sessions and don't worry about whether you're 'doing it right' or not. Just allow yourself to let go – this is one part of your training where trying too hard can be counterproductive.

At the end of the session, allow yourself to sit quietly for a few moments before carrying on with your normal activities.

2 Mental calmness

Mental calmness and physical relaxation are closely connected. When you are physically relaxed, your brain activity slows and you float down to alpha level. Here, your left brain is quiet and the critical censor which controls the passage of ideas into your unconscious during the waking state is numbed, so your mind is more receptive to your affirmations and mental imagery.

3 Creative imagery

In alpha state, you can use your battery of creative imagery techniques to place positive thoughts into your unconscious, record over your 'old tapes' and rehearse forthcoming events until they are second nature to you. You can also use anchoring to manage your emotional state and re-framing to deal with unhelpful memories from the past. Remember, although visualization is a very powerful way of imprinting your thoughts on the unconscious, you mustn't worry if you find it difficult to conjure up sharp images. Some people can actually 'see' things with crystal clarity but many others cannot and, if you are one of these, imagine, think, hear or sense the situation instead.

If distracting thoughts do occur, don't dwell on them. Release them by quietly saying the word 'relax' to yourself until they gently float away.

4 Positive self-talk

What you say to yourself matters, so make sure your self-talk is constructive. During the day, use thought stopping to eliminate negative self-talk before replacing it with positive 'mental nutrition'. Recite your affirmations at least ten times each, three times a day. When in alpha, either recite them to yourself (the process of directly re-programming the unconscious in this way is called autosuggestion) or record them on to a cassette tape and play the tape over and over again.

5 The 'as if' principle

There are two sides to the 'as if' principle. We've already touched on the first, which is best summed up as 'fake it 'til you make it'. The idea is simple enough: if you act *as if* you already are the kind of person you want to be, you will inevitably become that person. You'll find yourself performing better and will notice other people's response to the changes in you.

However, there is a second part which takes a little more explaining because we haven't mentioned it at all so far in this book. It involves imagining or believing that there is a greater sense of purpose to your sporting activities than winning alone. If this sounds a little far-fetched, read on.

Every society in the world believes that there must be a greater intelligence over-seeing us. Some call it God, others Krishna, Allah, the Great Spirit or Jehovah, but it doesn't really matter what you call it, as long as it works for you. We'll call it the 'Universal Intelligence'. Now imagine this Power taking care of you, tirelessly responding to your efforts, helping you to bring your dreams into reality.

We're not preaching any particular religion but it does seem to us that athletes who feel exalted by a sense of being part of a greater whole bring something to their sport which is often lacking in others. The athlete, Kriss Akabusi, claims that becoming a born-again Christian provided the inspiration which took him to Olympic success. He now gives talks to schools and works unceasingly for a variety of good causes. The multi-Olympic gold medallist, Carl Lewis has attributed much of his success to his faith. George Foreman, who retired from professional boxing to become a preacher, then returned to the ring and regained the World Heavyweight Championship at 46 years of age, attributed his success to his faith. So did Muhammad Ali later in his career. And Herb Elliot, the brilliant Australian runner who retired from the sport at 23 years of age, claimed that his spiritual beliefs enabled him to go into another dimension in which there were no limits on what he could achieve.

In the USA the Fellowship of Christian Athletes, founded in 1954, has helped many to fulfil their potential. Madeline Manning-Mimms, an Olympic gold medallist in Mexico in 1968 and chaplain to the US Olympic team, summed up her philosophy in the following words: 'Look inward – then you can look outward and be all you can be.' This is a universal doctrine by no means confined to the Christian tradition.

For you to benefit from the 'as if' principle, it doesn't really matter whether there is a Universal Intelligence at all. Look again at Dynamic Living Principle No. 1: 'You create your own reality with your thoughts, feelings and attitudes'. What is important is that *you believe there is*. If you have the belief that some magnificent force is taking care of you, you step out confidently, knowing that anything that happens is ultimately for your benefit. All you have to do is have faith in yourself and the Power that is working through you.

When we did our fire-walk (see page 37), the facilitator summed up the secret of success in life very simply:

- Be mindful.
- Expect the best.
- Go for it!

The recipe for winning at the game of life is now yours. All you have to do is combine the ingredients and savour the results. You'll be able to follow the example of the high-jump champion who was asked for the secret of his success. 'All I do,' he said, 'is throw my heart over the bar and the rest follows.' Health, happiness and success are yours for the taking – what are you waiting for?

Allow yourself to be guided and supported by the Universal Intelligence which is within you and you will always be healthy, happy and successful and have the courage to follow your dreams.

Dynamic Living Principle No. 10

Getting started: a 28-day programme

Many people tell us they want to use our techniques but wonder how to get started. 'There's too much in your book to do all at once,' they say. 'Can you suggest a step-by-step way to begin?'

For this reason, we've put together a 4-week programme which will point you in the right direction. We haven't included all our techniques and we would like to emphasize that merely doing this programme for 4 weeks and then stopping will not get you the results you want. So keep at it, and good luck!

You'll find these exercises on the audio cassette, *Decide to Win*, and the accompanying relaxation tape, *Relax and Decide to Win* (see page 142).

Week I

We're assuming you're already taking steps to improve your diet and are exercising as we've suggested. Now:

- Set your goals. Write them down. Write down all the benefits that will accrue to you when you achieve them. (See Chapter 3)

- Examine your beliefs. Write down your limiting beliefs, i.e. all the reasons why you think you can't achieve your goals. Then cross them out and replace them with the opposites, i.e. beliefs that you need to hold. (See Chapters 8 and 10)

- Decide on the qualities you need. List them. (See Chapter 2)

- Practise the complete breath. Use it to enhance your energy and calm you down when under stress. (See Chapter 7)

- Try out tensing and relaxing and autogenic relaxation and choose the one which works best for you. Experience alpha state for yourself every day. If you find this difficult, use a relaxation tape such as *Relax and Decide to Win*. (See Chapter 10)

Week 2

As for Week 1, plus:

- Continue with your relaxation. Practise moving quickly and easily between peak state and resting state. (See Chapter 5)

- Practise rhythmic breathing to help you relax more effectively. (See Chapter 7)

- Prioritize your goals and set deadlines. (See Chapter 3)

- Work on the belief that you can achieve your goal. Start by compiling affirmations to reinforce your new belief system and the qualities you need to acquire. Use them every day. (See Chapter 10)

- Take stock of your present situation. Identify any obstacles you will have to overcome and the resources you will need. (See Chapter 3)

- When relaxed, see or sense yourself already having the qualities you need and back this up with affirmations such as 'I am . . .' (See Chapter 10)

- Install an anchor that will get you into peak state at will. (See Chapter 12)

Week 3

As for Week 2, plus:

- Plan your physical and mental training programme. Write it down. (See Chapters 3 and 13)

- Use creative imagery to visualize yourself as if your goal were already achieved. (See Chapter 12)

- Practise positive self-talk. Notice whenever you are talking negatively to yourself and change it immediately. (See Chapter 12)

- Develop some empowering rituals to focus your mind and get you psyched up, ready for action. (See Chapter 13)

- Practise re-framing. Choose events which have influenced your belief system and re-interpret them. When in alpha, see them working out differently. (See Chapter 12)

Week 4

As for Week 3, plus:

- Place yourself on a seven-day mental diet and don't give up until you've accomplished it. (See Chapter 10)

- Practise managing your emotional state using physiology and re-focussing. (See Chapter 11)

- Use mental rehearsal to prepare you for a forthcoming event. It needn't be a sports fixture – any challenge you face will provide you with the practice you need and reassure you that the technique really works. Back it up with affirmations, such as 'I am a winner' or 'I play well and win the game'. (See Chapter 12)

- Practise the 'as if' principle. Think, talk and act as if you are a winner. Back it up with affirmations and creative imagery. Take notice of how it feels and anchor those feelings deeply into your nervous system so you can draw on them at will. (See Chapters 12 and 16)

The Dynamic Living Principles

A recipe for health, happiness and success

1 You create your own reality with your thoughts, feelings and attitudes.
2 You have the right to a better quality of life; to health, happiness and success.
3 The reason most people get ill is because their lives aren't working.
4 You can transform your life by changing your attitude.
5 Whatever your mind can conceive and believe, you can achieve.
6 Decide to build into yourself the qualities and characteristics you need for success.
7 You can have whatever you want in life, providing you are willing to invest the necessary time, energy and effort.
8 Live in the present moment. Life is a journey to be enjoyed, not a struggle to be endured.
9 Transform your conscious mind with the Dynamic Living Principles and your unconscious with the Dynamic Living Formula.
10 Allow yourself to be guided and supported by the Universal Intelligence which is within you and you will always be healthy, happy and successful and have the courage to follow your dreams.

Further Information

The authors are co-founders of the Dynamic Living Institute and the Dynamic Sports Institute, where they teach ways of improving the quality of life and improving sporting performance. Information, advice and sound practical techniques are relayed in talks, seminars and workshops, as well as by individual counselling. The Sports Institute caters for both teams and individuals.

In addition to books and pamphlets, the following may be obtained:

- *Dynamic Living Programme* This is made up of l2 units, covering every aspect of happy and successful living, from mind power and positive thinking to stress management, communication skills and relationships. Each unit consists of: a 60-minute instructional tape; a relaxation tape, which works at an unconscious level; informative study notes; and exercises to help you speed your progress.

- *Decide to Win* A motivational tape which complements this book and which you can listen to at any time, especially when you are on your way to a game and want to arrive in a positive frame of mind.

- *Relax and Decide to Win* A relaxation tape which will help you to ingrain the winning habit deeply into your mind.

For further details, contact the Institute in question at:

45A Branksome Wood Road
Bournemouth Dorset BH4 9JT
UK
Tel. 01202 762202

Please enclose a stamped addressed (A4 size) envelope.

Index